INTRODUCTION
TO THE
OCCULT

BOOKS BY RICHARD SMOLEY

INTRODUCTION
TO THE
OCCULT

*Your guide to subjects ranging from
Atlantis, magic, and UFOs to witchcraft,
psychedelics, and thought power*

RICHARD SMOLEY

&
MEDIA

Published 2022 by Gildan Media LLC
aka G&D Media
www.GandDmedia.com

First Edition: 2022

Front cover design by Tom McKeveny

Interior design by Meghan Day Healey of Story Horse, LLC.

Library of Congress Cataloging-in-Publication Data is available upon request

ISBN: 978-1-7225-0589-9

10 9 8 7 6 5 4 3 2 1

Contents

1

Knowledge

Welcome to this book. It's about the occult—the magic that has to do with unseen worlds. This could open up the most exciting adventure of your life, and possibly the most important.

You may have picked up this book because you have a sense of something much larger than yourself, much larger even than the world we see. In his play *Our Town*, Thornton Wilder has one of his characters say, "Now there are some things we all know, but we don't take'm out and look at'm very often. We all know that *something* is eternal. And it ain't houses and it ain't names, and it ain't earth, and it ain't even the stars... everybody knows in their bones that *something* is eternal, and that something has to do with human beings.... There's something way down deep that's eternal about every human being."

It's possible, even likely, that you are reading this book because you have this intuition.

Occult means *hidden*. This is one of the many different meanings to this term.

Have you ever seen a pond that was completely covered with green scum? It practically looks like a lawn. If you did not know anything more about that pond, you would think that the scum on the surface was everything instead of merely the thin surface of a much larger body of water.

I'd like to suggest to you that this is what the universe is like. Everything we see, everything we hear, from the tiniest submicroscopic particles to galaxies millions of light years away, is simply the surface.

We know that this physical world is merely the surface. We know there is much, much more. That is what all of the great religions, all of the great philosophies, throughout time from prehistory to now, have known and tried to tell us.

Many people today are suspicious of religion and religious forms. It's partly because religion can catch you in the trap of thinking that the forms—the doctrines, rituals, scriptures—are the ultimate truth. They aren't. They're merely paths to the truth.

In this book, I want to give you some idea of what lies under all of these externals. It can be approached through any of the religious paths—as long as the path does not pretend it's the only path—or without any of them.

A verse in the New Testament says, "Woe unto you, scribes and Pharisees, hypocrites! For ye shut up the gate of the kingdom of heaven against men: for ye neither go in yourselves, neither suffer ye them that are entering to go in" (Matthew 23:13). That can happen with religion. If you focus too much on the scriptures, the doctrines, the literal facts, you are staying on the surface. If you are a religious leader, you run the risk of keeping others from going deeper as well.

In this respect, we live in a very fortunate time, because many of these religious forms have lost their power, and people are opening up to the possibility of truth beyond these forms. Many people describe themselves these days as spiritual but not religious. They often mean that they have some intuition of this greater depth but are not satisfied with the religious concepts they're presented with.

Some claim that we can approach the whole truth about the universe through science. Science often acts as if it's telling us the whole truth, but it doesn't. It's actually a very limited form of inquiry. To pretend that everything we know can be summed up scientifically is a great error.

It has caused as much suffering as religious persecutions and wars.

There is a deeper reality, and I would like to help you explore it. I have some experience in these areas. I've reflected on them for decades. I've written eleven books and spoken to many people, so I have some insights. I'm willing to share them with you, but I can't pretend to be telling you the whole truth, because I don't know the whole truth. Nobody does. The whole truth is vaster and more sublime than our minds can approach, but we can approach it a little more closely than we may have.

I'm going to tell you the truth about a lot of mysterious subjects as I understand them. It's important to steer a middle course between skepticism—"it's all bunk. It's all been debunked"—and total credulity: "Yes, it's all true. Wow. I believe everything I see or hear about mystical subjects."

Neither of those is a sensible approach. In some ways, when you start looking into the unseen worlds, you have to be more critical than in ordinary life, because there's always the capacity for self-illusion and self-deception. That possibility has always got to be in the background, if not the forefront, of your mind. On the other hand, if you compulsively doubt, saying, "It's all nonsense," that too is a trap.

At this point, I need to say something else that I think is extremely important. It's quite possible that many or most or all of the people you know and love are not interested in this kind of knowledge and in one way or another oppose it. You may have hyperreligious people in your life who insist that their way is the only way, and if you don't follow it, you're going to fall into the clutches of the Devil. (I will talk about the Devil and what the Devil might mean later.)

You may well find that people around you are unsympathetic. Most people are simply not interested in these things. It's true of most of my friends. I'm talking about people who are educated and intelligent, often far wealthier and far more successful than I am in worldly terms. Yet they have no more interest in these subjects than my dog. This is not a problem in our friendship, because we can simply talk about something else. But the fact that your friends or family do not necessarily share your interests does not mean that these interests are not valid or true. It means that you have to know when to talk about them and when not to talk about them, and whom to talk about them with and whom *not* to talk about them with.

The magical path is summed up in four aphorisms: *to know, to will, to dare,* and *to be silent.* I suggest that the last one is the most important. You have to know when to keep your mouth shut. Actually, it's true in any area of life. You know it's true at work. You know that with your spouse or significant other, there are times when you'd better keep your lip zipped up or your relationship is going to suffer. The same is true with these matters.

Nevertheless, it is possible to find people who are interested in these subjects: like-minded souls. It's probably easier to find them than it has ever been, if only because social media give us access to enormous numbers of people, so you can have a virtual network of friends with the same interests. Things are a lot less lonely than they were even a couple of decades ago.

If you continue to investigate the spiritual side of things, you will probably gravitate more and more toward people with the same interests. Your current interests could also lose some of their appeal. You may no longer be able to be so upset when your sports team loses. People may even look at you and say, "You're starting to become a bit colorless," because you don't share their enthusiasms.

To speak frankly—and I will do my best to speak frankly throughout this book—that is a risk you have to run. You may also run the risk of losing interest in many of the people and activities that surround you. In the end, you will gain much more than you gave up.

By the way, here's another mystical secret: you can never give up what's true. The only things you can give up are illusions. We live in a world of illusions. We live in a world that tries to make us believe that certain things are more important than they are, or that we should be terribly excited or upset about the most insignificant matters. We are not likely to change this fact about the world, but we can say, "Maybe this isn't so important after all. Maybe I shouldn't get so upset about these things. Maybe I need to find a center in myself from which I can observe all the world's doing. Maybe I can avoid becoming a cold, detached, hard-hearted person, but I can still live with others and behave decently with them without being submerged in upsets and concerns."

That is one benefit that I hope you'll take away from this book. I very much look forward to having you continue this journey with me.

2

Mindfulness

What if I told you that you are asleep right now? Sitting here, reading this book, you are asleep.

How could that be? We think of sleep in terms of nighttime and daytime. You go to bed and you have two forms of sleep: dreamless sleep and sleep with dreams. Then there's waking life. Is that consciousness? In a way, because throughout any given day you can perform any number of extraordinarily complex actions and decisions. It takes enormous mental and physical coordination simply to enter a highway in your car. This is consciousness of a kind.

Nonetheless, much of this waking consciousness is automatic, even mechanical. We use this idea in ordinary language: we say, "I was on autopilot." You are doing something while you are thinking something completely different, so there's a detachment between what's going on in your mind and what your body's doing.

This disjuncture is a kind of sleep. The great mystical philosopher G.I. Gurdjieff even said that it is the sleep of man. Here's what he may have meant.

An ancient teaching, which goes back at least as far as Plato, says that we are composed of three elements: the body, the emotions, and the mind. We are tripartite beings. It may be the case that the connections between these parts aren't as close as they might be. You will find people who don't know what their own feelings are: there's little if any connection between their mind and their emotions. Furthermore, we often perform many actions capably while our minds are completely focused on something else. Driving is a perfect example. Your body is executing all sorts of complex motions while your mind is drifting away toward what you have to do tomorrow, how fond you are or are not of your boss, your relations with your loved ones, and so on. This could be called a kind of sleep—a waking sleep.

Part of the spiritual path is to bring all of these centers—mind, body, and emotions—a little closer together. You may well find that you are not comfortable in one of these areas as in the others. You may be a great athlete or artist who can barely think. We are all familiar with the stock figure of the absent-minded professor.

Mindfulness points toward an integration of these three parts of the self. To begin with, you need to see what's going on in yourself. When is the best time to see this? Now.

You will hear an enormous amount about being present, being mindful, being in the moment, and the power of now. All of these messages are important and powerful. Actually, they were quite esoteric until fairly recently; now they're on the lips of everyone. There are corporate seminars on mindfulness (good or bad, I don't know; I've never been to one). This idea is out there. It's a valuable one to take seriously, because you can only know really what's going on in you in a given moment.

There are many mindfulness practices. Some of them involve meditation, which I'll get to in the next chapter, but many of them can and should be carried out in daily life as often as possible. This requires great discipline. It will seem very difficult at first, but when you learn how to walk, it also seemed very difficult, and you mastered that.

Let me give you a simple exercise. While you're reading this book, pay attention to what I'm saying while having a sensation of your feet on the floor (or wherever they are). See if you can feel your feet while reading. What do they feel like now, right in this moment? Until I mentioned it, you probably were not aware in the moment that you even had feet. Maybe you knew it in the background, but what is it like now? What do your feet feel like now?

Quite likely if you try to keep a part of your attention on your feet while you reading, you will gradually drift off—not necessarily to sleep, but you'll lose touch with one or the other: you'll forget your feet, or you'll stop paying attention to your reading. Why? Because the mind and the body are not as closely connected as they could be.

This kind of greater connection or integration is extremely important for functioning in life. It is a prerequisite to having a successful life in any genuine sense of that term.

How do you integrate your mind, your emotions, and your body? Minimally, by being aware of them. Being aware in this way may point up some conflict. You might find that you've just had a good meal or a cup of coffee, and your body feels fine, but your emotions feel quite different. They may be agitated or angry. That's going to happen. The point is not to feel any particular way; rather it's to know what is going on, what you are feeling, and what you are thinking.

Many mindfulness practices can be used in daily life. Here's a simple one. Try it for the next week. Every time you touch a doorknob, feel your hand touching the doorknob. You don't have to touch it any differently. (As you can see, this does not take an extra second out of your day, so you can't pretend that you don't have time.) See what happens. Even make a note for yourself: "A week from now, I will look back on my experience with consciously sensing doorknobs. How many times did I remember? How many times did I forget?" Most of the time, you'll probably have forgotten.

Funnily enough, the first step to what is sometimes called *self-remembering* is to realize that you've forgotten, just as the first step toward knowledge is to know that you don't know. If you don't know but you think you know, you're lost. If you don't know but you realize that, you have a chance to find out. You have a chance to learn.

There's a famous story about the Greek philosopher Socrates. Someone sent to the oracle at Delphi, which predicted the future. It was held in the highest regard: states consulted it to decide whether they should go to war. The oracle was asked who was the wisest man in Greece. The oracle said, "Socrates." When Socrates heard that, he said, "I have no idea of what it could possibly mean, except that I realize that I don't know. Everybody else is going around thinking they know."

To begin with, mindfulness means being aware of your constant forgetting. As I said, there are many other practices for this. I've given you two. One is to be aware when you're touching the doorknob. The other is simply feel your feet on the floor (or wherever they are) whenever you think of it. What happens if you feel your feet on the floor while you're taking a shower? What will change? Something will change, but I'm not going to tell you what, because you have to discover it for yourself—and anyway, what you discover might be quite different from what I think it might be.

Here's another powerful practice. This leads into meditation, which I'll deal with in the next chapter. It's to remember the breath. You're breathing; you'd better be breathing, or you're not going to be around much longer. All right, what is it like? How am I breathing? Can I feel the breath go in and out? Am I taking long breaths, short breaths, tense breaths? The psychologist Fritz Perls said that anxiety is holding the breath. You may notice that when you're anxious, you'll hold the breath for a second or two before letting it out. That is an expression of tension; it also contributes to tension.

Mindfulness practiced properly should lead to greater relaxation and comfort, even if the first thing you notice is tension, because, again, if you know you're tense, now you know that you can relax. When you didn't know you were tense, you didn't have the option.

These are some very simple concepts and steps, but mindfulness is at the start of this book because it is among the most important things in it.

3

Meditation

Meditation, like many things that I'm discussing, was once a highly esoteric topic: few people knew anything about it. If they did, they thought of it as exotic, something done by holy men in the East.

Over the last fifty or sixty years, the situation has changed. There is an enormous amount of information about meditation, including many forms of instruction available.

If you really want to develop internally along the lines that I'm talking about here, meditation is important. Integrating this practice into your life will make a huge difference. You don't have to start out meditating for a half hour a day (a common length of time). You can start out doing it for five or ten minutes. Some people have a great deal of difficulty sitting still, and five or ten minutes to them is an eternity. That's fine. You have to know your limits, but even the act of choosing to sit in meditation for five to ten minutes involves a conscious decision: you've decided to make time for this in your life. Conscious decision and commitment come from yourself internally: "I am going to incorporate this into my day."

Why would you decide to take up meditation? Everybody is too busy; everybody has too much to do; everybody is doing half a dozen things at a time (usually none of them particularly well). Why should I make this kind of time for myself? What good will it do me?

Let me go back to something I mentioned in the first chapter. Like every human being, I believe, you have an intuition of something far greater than yourself. You're probably a little different, because you're aware of this fact and you want to bring this greater reality into your life, even though you don't necessarily know how.

How do you engage with the great waters of reality that live under the green scum that is the world of the five senses? How do you bring yourself to deal with this hidden dimension? Meditation is one way, because it brings you into your own deeper levels, of which you are normally not aware.

Bringing yourself consciously into these deeper levels at a specific time of the day is very helpful. As I say, the conscious decision to do this and the constant practice of it are in themselves a huge step, because they involve inner discipline. Discipline is not a popular word, but from the point of view of what we're talking about, it's absolutely essential.

Why? For one thing, you will probably not get much social support for your interest or your activities. You may find your loved ones unsympathetic and even threatened by your interests. Another verse out of the New Testament: "And a man's foes shall be those of his own household" (Matthew 10:36). That's what this verse is talking about. If you are—to use Christian terms—seeking the kingdom of God (which I will discuss in a later chapter), your family and friends are very likely not going to be interested in it. Even if they think they are, their concepts of what it is and what will get you there are more likely to hurt than help you.

You have to have the discipline to make a space in yourself for the spirit in spite of the world, in spite of everything. Can you do this? I don't know. You have to answer this for yourself. If you want to become a truly authentic human being, this is an important step, not because I say so, but because it *is* so. I don't know everything and don't pretend to, but these ideas and principles are universal and time-tested.

Ideally, it's best to learn meditation from a qualified instructor—someone who has experience with that particular practice and can teach it to you and with whom you can discuss how it's going later on. That is the ideal. Meditation is taught in a wide variety of places and under a wide variety of names. Which is the best? The one you're most drawn to, the one that you think will work for you, at least initially. If it doesn't, then you find another.

Meditation is a way of drawing yourself deeper into this ocean of reality that lies inside you and that, by the way, you really *are*. People say, "I don't really know who I am," or "I'm trying to find myself." What an absurd question! That should be the easiest thing to answer, yet it's the most difficult. Why? Here's a possibility. You *are* this great ocean of being. You are *that* much more than you are your personality or identity, your social status, or your wealth, but if you're not aware of this fact, you feel that you don't you know who you are. In a sense, you don't. Meditation connects you with that inner depth.

Thanks to Buddhism, the concept of enlightenment has become very common today. Many people think of it rather materialistically as a thing you get. No. It's not a Maserati. It's not even a college degree. It is a process. Contact with this ocean of being is a kind of enlightenment. But don't fool yourself into thinking there's a stopping place. Never forget that there's always further to go, even though you may stop at a certain point and rest for a while.

Here's another verse from the Bible: "In my Father's house, there are many mansions" (John 14:2). In the Greek in which the New Testament was written, that word doesn't really mean *mansions*. It means *way stations*: places where you stop along the way. You will encounter way stations in spiritual practice. That's all well and good, but a way station isn't home. You're not moving into that motel; you've checked in for one night. You rest there, and you go on. There's always further to go.

One familiar type of meditation is the mantra meditation. A mantra or mantram—both forms are used— is a sacred syllable or name that you repeat constantly and silently in meditative practice, and which will draw you deeper into that ocean of being. The Hindu traditions have many mantras. In the Jewish Kabbalah, the Hebrew names of God are used as mantras. Jews are not supposed to say the name of God aloud. Similarly, some meditation practices will tell you never to tell your mantra to anybody. Why? Because it's a meditation word. You take it to follow it deeper into yourself. Saying it aloud sucks the power out of it.

Another type of meditation, which is very common in Buddhism, uses the breath. It goes back to the Buddha himself. He said, "If you're taking a long breath, be aware that you're taking a long breath. If you're taking a short breath, be aware that you're taking a short breath." Much Buddhist meditative practice is focused on contemplating the breathing. That's a practice you can do right off. Again, I would suggest competent instruction by a qualified teacher, but you can simply try it on your own, just as I've given it.

You sit quietly with your back straight. You don't need to sit in an elaborate cross-legged position, but it is helpful to have the back straight: meditation is rest, but it's not sleep.

Sit in a chair with your back straight. Close your eyes quietly, and allow your attention to rest on the breath for five, ten, fifteen minutes, a half hour. You're not controlling the breath; you're not hyperventilating or deep breathing. You observe the breath as it is. You watch it objectively and compassionately. That's a deep lesson in itself.

This is one simple practice. I would suggest doing it at any hour of the day when you can be left alone and your mind is reasonably quiet. Generally it's a good idea to have a specific time of day for meditation.

I don't think you should have to pay enormous amount to learn meditation. Most of the best teachers of meditation I know of teach it for free. Why? Here's one reason: the things that are valuable in the real world, the world of the ocean of being, have no value in terms of the world of the surface, and vice versa.

4

Love

When people think of love, they often ask, will I find the perfect partner? if they haven't already (and sometimes even if they have). This is true regardless of your sex or sexual orientation. If you feel you haven't, it can feel very lonely indeed.

Let me give you a reassuring answer. Yes, you can find a life partner that's suited to you. Most do. The vast majority of people get married at some point or another in their lives, so we can assume that there's someone for you; you'll find that person, if you haven't already. This doesn't come out of any uncanny prophetic powers on my part; it's merely statistical likelihood. When, where, and how—those are things I can't tell you, of course.

Let's say you find your perfect partner. That problem is solved; it can be checked off the list. You settle down. Let's say you have children. As my father-in-law said to me when my first son was born, "Now it begins." Suddenly, one problem, which you've solved—finding the perfect partner—transforms into the problem of family life. It's not all bad, of course, but I've met few people who ever said it was easy. Indeed life has a peculiar way of replacing one solved problem with another in short order.

At any rate, there is sexual, romantic love, which (ideally) culminates in marriage. Sexual, romantic, and marital love are all on a continuum. There are, of course, many other forms of love: friendship, family love, and something higher, which Christians call *agape*, which is the word for *love* usually used in the Greek New Testament.

I want to break down love into two fundamental categories. One is *transactional love*. It covers just about everything that I've discussed up to now. Although it may sound cold to say this, even the most intimate forms of love have a transactional element in them—and they should.

Take the case of a woman who's abused by her husband. Every night for the last twenty years, he's gotten drunk and kicked her down the stairs. Her friends ask, "Why don't you leave?" She replies, "I love him." That sounds a little funny. Her friends might tell her, "Look. You've got to get out of there before he kills you." Modern terminology calls this not love but codependence.

There are transactions in marital love. Both parties have to honor certain commitments, such as a minimal decency of behavior—not to abuse or hurt your partner. The same is true with friendship. It's the most common thing in the world to say, "You know, honey, we've invited those people five times for dinner, and they've never invited us." "Yes, let's just give them up."

The friendship may be warm and genuine up to a point, but if it's not reciprocated, it's not going to go anywhere. Nor should it. People who fulfill their end of the bargain even when the other person doesn't start to be seen as losers. They seem needy or pathetic, and with some reason.

Family love is often thought of as the purest love there is. What finer love can there be than the love of a mother for her child? Even here, although the transactional element is in the background, it isn't completely missing. In the first place, the mother loves the child because it is *her* child. She may love this child no matter what this child grows up to do, but it is totally contingent upon its being *her* child. In the second place, it's understood that a parent of small children is going to be all about giving, not getting; in the long run, though, there is some expectation that when the parents are old and frail, the kids are going to be around to help them out.

There's nothing wrong with these forms of transactionality, but people become confused and unhappy when they believe that transactional love is unconditional when it's nothing of the kind. When a couple starts dating, often one of them will say, "I don't care how this relationship works out. I just want what's best for her." Six weeks later, they've had a fight, they've broken up, and both parties wish each other dead.

This kind of thing happens more often than you can count, so you have to be a bit cynical about it. In fact, much of the world deserves a bit of cynicism. At the same time, we need to go beyond cynicism. A lot of what goes on is a joke, but not everything else is a joke.

Let me go on to conscious love, which, I believe, is unconditional love. (My book *Conscious Love* goes into this subject in depth.) Conscious love should not be mistaken for sentimentality. Although it's good, it's not necessarily warm. It not only wishes the best for the other person, but also knows what's best, no matter how it may look at the moment. At the highest level, under certain circumstances certain spiritual teachers act in odd and counterintuitive ways. This may be because they are seeing what's necessary rather than what people think should be necessary.

I don't want to draw hard and fast lines between transactional and unconditional love. They blend into each other, and they should, because that's human life. But it's a good idea not to mistake one for the other.

For day-to-day life, I'm going to use a simple, old-fashioned, rather boring word, which is *decency*. Ordinary human decency. We're not talking about love; we're not talking about compassion. We're not talking about any of the grand words that we use to inspire and frequently delude ourselves with.

Decency is plain, vanilla, unadorned. That is its precise value. What's the decent thing to do? Sometimes letting someone get ahead of you in traffic in the decent thing to do. Is it going to get you points in heaven? Maybe; maybe not.

All this is obvious, and it should be. I'm not going to explain ordinary human decency, because I believe you already know what it is. But I want to point out one particular advantage: sometimes your decency is your only protection. There is an old saying, which was the title of a W. C. Fields movie back in the thirties: "You can't cheat an honest man." Why? Because scams are based on getting the victim to think he's scamming somebody else. A decent person wouldn't do that, so a decent person can't be cheated. Moreover, a decent person won't retaliate. If everybody lived by this principle, many of the spirals of enmity and hatred and vindictiveness that occur in life wouldn't happen. A decent person simply lets the offense go. On the other hand, such a person does not serve as a doormat; at times he or she will have to say, "Goodbye; I don't want any more part of this."

Your decency will protect you from many of the mistakes you could make and from much unhappiness. If you deal with people this way on the street, in your relationships, in your workplace, life will be better and easier. It won't always be easy, because life is never always easy, but ordinary decency will prevent a lot of the problems that we sometimes take for granted. It may be the single most important thing to remember about love.

5

The Colors of Magic

Like lots of words, *magic* has a number of meanings. One is stage magic, sleight of hand magic, where you pull a quarter out from behind someone's ear or a rabbit out of a hat. Some of these tricks can be incredibly elaborate and impressive, but they have nothing to do with occult magic. I'm not going to talk about sleight of hand magic and stage magic, because I don't know about them. You would have to go to somebody else for that.

I think I can talk a little bit about the other kind of magic—occult magic, as it's called, about which there is an enormous number of preconceptions and miscon-ceptions. Let me try to set some of them straight.

Although I just said that there were two differ-ent types of magic—sleight of hand magic and occult magic—often people try to pass one off as the other, sometimes quite elaborately. There are mentalists who have their assistants go through the audience, find out certain facts about people, and then transmit them to the mentalist, who then "mystically" knows where a given person comes from. That's entertaining if you're doing it for entertainment. It's shoddy if you're doing it to induce religious belief.

In any case, the overlap exists. The fraud exists. What, then, is real magic, occult magic? As we've seen, *occult* means *hidden*—in this particular sense, hidden from our ordinary senses. You're dealing here with forces that are not generally understood or explained or accepted.

Occult magic is sometimes said to effect changes through paranormal means. Does it work? Yes, it does, or can, work. So why doesn't everybody use it? Because it is almost impossible to employ it without unexpected and undesired side effects.

A friend of mine had a boyfriend who was starting a business. He needed $10,000 to get it started, so she did a magical working to get him the money. At that time, she was finishing medical school and moving out of her dorm. After she had her belongings loaded into her car, it was broken into, and everything was stolen. The insurance settlement came to—guess what?—$10,000.

There's an old joke in which a man gets a magic bottle that has a genie in it. He rubs the bottle, and the genie appears and says, "All right. You now have three wishes." The man says, "OK. Well, make me a hamburger." The genie obligingly turns him into a hamburger. Although this is a rather stupid joke, it does have some wisdom. You have to be careful of what you ask for.

Part of my task here is to free you of some of the illusions that you've gotten from Hollywood horror movies about the occult, because of course these versions are all sensationalized—blood spurting from the ceiling, murderous clowns lurking in sewers. Does it work that way? Not really. Scriptwriters seem to think that everything has to be grossly overstated, including horror.

We often hear about black magic. Generally speaking, black magic has two aims. Sometimes it's to hurt someone else. At other times it's meant to make someone do something against their will. A classic case of the latter is getting a person to fall in love with you. There are all sorts of spells going back to classical antiquity and beyond for this purpose. In a word, this is unethical. It also generally leads to adverse results. One wit quipped, "Love magic works only on its practitioner, and in reverse."

Another kind of black magic is done to harm someone else. This has long been common. I recently read a book about witchcraft in England over the last two hundred years. (It's called *Cursed Britain: A History of Witchcraft and Black Magic in Modern Times*, by Thomas Waters.) There's been plenty of it. Many cases took place in rural contexts—for example, casting a spell that will cause a person's cows to dry up. This may not sound serious to today's urbanite, but this was not a world where you went to the store and got milk for $2.69 a gallon. Milk was your livelihood.

Did these practices work? I don't know, but it is strange to see how many different cases are reported that are remarkably similar, even though the victims had no idea of any other ones. Often they didn't even know what was happening at first.

Skeptics say, "Magic has to do with suggestion. It's a matter of belief. If you believe in magic, you're going to be susceptible to it." This isn't satisfactory. In many cases, these effects happened to people who didn't believe in magic or didn't even know that a spell was cast. In fact, it's standard practice to make sure that victims *don't* know the spell has been cast, because then they can take countermeasures. Simplistic rationalism doesn't explain these phenomena, so we have to talk about how magic might work, which I'll do in the next few chapters.

Then there's white magic. Does this have racial implications? No. Admittedly, white is considered good and black is considered bad, but there is no racial associations or overtones to these terms; they've simply been used throughout the years.

White magic has a good purpose. In the old days, there were two kinds of witches. The ones that were called witches were those who practiced black magic. But there were also people who used this magic to help others; they were called *cunning men* or *cunning women*. That was the name for them. They would allegedly break others' spells, so their work had a good purpose. They might also perform magical practices to heal someone or to break a streak of bad luck.

Magic with an ambiguous purpose—performed chiefly out of with self-interest—is sometimes called *gray magic*. This is probably the most common kind, simply because we humans are a mixture of good and evil: we work from mixed motives.

Let's say you want a perfect love partner. With black magic, you would decide who that was and cast a spell on that person. Sometimes the techniques are quite funny. One way of trapping a man, according to one of these traditions, is for a woman is to dab a little menstrual blood behind each ear before a date. (Maybe it isn't as stupid as it sounds; after all, menstrual blood carries pheromones.) With gray magic, you might cast a spell to attract your perfect partner. You are not try-ing to manipulate a particular person, so black magic is not involved; instead you are seeking someone who presumably wants the same thing you do. Your goal is selfish but not harmful. White magic, by contrast, is performed for benevolent purposes, such as healing, breaking curses, or simply to attract benign forces.

Magic is part of the ocean of being that lies under the surface of superficial reality. It's not the whole, but it is another slice.

6

The Life Force

As we've seen, magic involves forces that most people don't know about. In this chapter I'm going to talk about one of these forces.

Everybody knows that there is an enormous difference between a living person and a corpse. What makes the difference? It's something called *life*. Although scientists talk a great deal about the properties of life and living things, they're vague about what life actually is.

I had a girlfriend years ago who had a cat. She watched the cat die. Both my girlfriend and her daughter said they could feel or notice something actually leaving when it died. That something is what I'm going to call the *life force.* There are huge numbers of names for it worldwide. Why? Because if this force exists, it must exist universally, and many people in many circumstances will have discovered it and given their own names to it. Because, for complex and perhaps inexplicable reasons, the modern scientific world doesn't believe in it, there's no real name for it in our culture, so I'm going to go on calling it the *life force.* In other cultures, you will hear it given many different names, for example, *prana* in India, *chi* or *qi* in China.

Certain scientists in the West have discovered this force and its properties. In the mid-nineteenth century a German scientist named Karl Ludwig von Reichenbach called it the *Odic force.* In the twentieth century, the Austrian psychiatrist Wilhelm Reich called it *orgone,* because he believed it was the energy released in the orgasm. But mainstream science has not accepted their findings.

Nonetheless, this force exists. It is in us. It is what makes us alive. It's the power that keeps you going. At some point, for reasons that are maybe clear, maybe not so clear, this force runs out or leaves, and that is what we call death.

This force can be generated and used in certain ways. Let's talk about it in a medical context. No doubt you've heard of acupuncture. Acupuncture is a traditional Chinese medical system that is still used today, and increasingly in the United States. It's thousands of years old. Used by a competent practitioner, it does work.

Acupuncture operates on the premise that the life force—chi—circulates in the body in a specific and precise way. It can be charted just as your circulatory system and nervous system can be charted. If you go to an acupuncturist's office, you'll see a big poster on the wall with a map of these lines of force, called *meridians*.

Acupuncture works on the premise that sometimes the flow of chi is obstructed or diverted: there's too much of it in one part of the system and not enough in another. There are a number of techniques for regulating the flow of chi, one of which is by sticking little needles into you. The needles go in about an eighth of an inch deep, or less. Although they produce a little sensation, it really doesn't hurt. This practice can achieve remarkable results. Doctors have used it to anesthetize patients—preventing them from feeling pain in some part of their body that is being cut into. That is only one of the many uses of acupuncture, and only one of many applications of the power of chi.

We have access to this power, because we have it going through our system. Under certain circumstances, you can actually feel the flow of this energy in your body. It moves around like a current, a channel. Sometimes these currents are called *winds*, because they can feel like winds moving around inside you.

The chakra system, which comes to us from Hinduism, is similar. Chakras (the name comes from the Sanskrit for *wheel*) are centers of energy that run up and down the middle of the body. There's one in your throat, your heart region, your solar plexus, the center of your forehead. You'll see diagrams of the chakras, often portrayed as lotuses of different colors.

The skeptic thinks, "How ridiculous!" because no doctor is going to cut up a person, living or dead, and find a little lotus near the heart. But nobody believes they would. Chakras and chi are not entities that a medical student will come across when dissecting a corpse; in fact, they are absent from a corpse. But with a certain amount of sensitivity and development, you can feel these systems in your own body. Certain types of meditation are used for this purpose.

These forces and systems are in the living body as it is sensed and perceived from within. That is why the charts of the chi meridians and chakras bear so little resemblance to the anatomy books studied in medical school. Both are valid views of the body, each from its own perspective. The view from one does not refute the view from another.

As a matter of fact, there are always many angles by which anything can be viewed. This includes reality itself, which is much wider, broader, and more mysterious than we can imagine. The fact that something looks one way from a particular perspective should not convince you that it does not look that way from another.

This life force is generated naturally in the body; you wouldn't be alive if it weren't. There are also certain ways of extending it out of your body. Here is a supposition: it's extremely common to feel someone's eyes on the back of your head. You don't have eyes on the back of your head, so you're not seeing anything, but you are perceiving *something*. You may be feeling the subtle flow of this energy, directed by the other person's attention. The fact that it's from another human heightens the interest, because your system is designed to respond to the things that are most important in your life, and another human's attention to you can be extremely important, whether that person is a potential lover or a potential killer.

That is one way we perceive the life force. Here's another way: the dirty look, the stink eye. If you've experienced this, you're not just responding to the other person's facial expression. You're feeling something from them: a sensation of a certain energy coming from the eyes. Our culture regards this as mild and harmless (when it pays attention to it at all). Other cultures don't always it see that way; some call it the *evil eye* and believe that it can cause real harm. Our word *envy* comes from the Latin *invidia*, which originally meant *evil eye*. In some societies, particularly in the Mediterranean region, it's believed that a certain type of person can put a curse on you just by looking at you, intentionally or not. I myself don't know if that's true, but I think there's something in the general principle: you're responding to a certain type of energy that is directed by someone's attention.

That's the bad side of it. The good side is when you meet a person you're attracted to, and something starts to flow; you just feel it. If the sexual attraction is mutual, it will be felt by both parties, whether they want to admit it or not. This happens with some people and not with others, which is a big subject in its own right.

What does this all have to do with magic? If this chi, this prana, this life force is something that you have and you can work it up in yourself, you can turn it to certain ends. You can make it do certain things, again for good or for evil.

The *Star Wars* movies reflect this concept when they speak of the Force. This is the force they're talking about. Those movies are so powerful in part because they're speaking of something that actually exists. As you'll remember from those films, the Force has a light side and a dark side. Like electricity, it is morally neutral. It can be used for any and all ends whatsoever. What you do with it depends on you.

The flow of this force goes on constantly. Your task in awakening is to become more sensitive to it, because it will enable you to see and know a lot of things that usually go completely over people's heads.

If you want to do something with this force, what do you do? You have to put it in some form. You have to direct it toward some aim. This is where the next concept in magic comes in.

7

The Astral Light

Like the life force, the subject of this chapter is an entity that science does not acknowledge; nonetheless, it exists. I'm going to use the traditional term for it: the *astral light*. Later I will explain why it has this name.

What is the substance of a thought? What is a thought made of? You have an image in your mind. Images come and go constantly, both in waking life and in the dream state. You experience them as flow. The most everyday thing that flows is water. Therefore *water* is one of the most universal metaphors for the substance that I'm talking about.

Under most circumstances, the things that flow through your mind, your thoughts and ideas, are ephemeral. They come and go. They have no force. You remember a dog that somebody walked in front of your house yesterday. You remember some image from a TV show. You remember the face of your first girlfriend or boyfriend. You can have many emotional reactions to these, but the thoughts themselves come and go. In fact, watching these thoughts come and go is itself a form of meditation.

Let's take one of these thoughts and see what we can do with it. If you take a thought, concentrate on it, and elaborate on it in your mind, it will start to have much more substance and power. Why? Because of the life force, chi. You're directing life force toward this mental image, in a sense feeding it. This process too is morally neutral. It could involve a beneficent, high-minded thought or the lowest, basest, cruelest thought. The process works either way.

This is one major key to the practice of magic. You take a thought, and you focus on it. You devote energy to it. The most common way of doing this is by intense visualization. This is a learned skill. If you really want to do something with magic, you have to train your mind. One way of doing this is to keep your mind trained on a single thought or image.

This is easiest to do if you have an object in front of you. Say you want to visualize a flame. Sit in front of a lit candle, close your eyes, and visualize this candle with the flame. When this image starts to slip from your mind, open your eyes, look at the flame, and start all over again.

This is a type of mental gymnastics that, at its core, is no different from physical gymnastics. It's a matter of acquiring skill and strength. The more you increase the power of your mental imaging, the more you can focus your chi on a particular mental form, the stronger it will be.

This effect can be heightened by magical ritual. The magician performs certain rites (sometimes taken from old books, sometimes self-devised) employing gestures, chants, and magical signs called sigils. These rites can be extremely simple or complex, depending on the practitioner's tastes and expectations.

Let me bring in another piece of theory here. According to the esoteric teachings, the world works in the opposite way to the way we normally think it does. Materialism tells us that thoughts are merely side-effects of brain activity: the physical comes first. But according to occult theory, everything that exists has a prior form in this astral light, as a mental image, before manifesting in the physical world.

In short, if you visualize something powerfully, perhaps heightening the effect through ritual, it may manifest in physical form. Of course this can have all sorts of repercussions. It is, again, extraordinarily difficult to make this manifestation occur without undesired side effects. This should lead one, I would hope, to be careful about using any magical rites, no matter what their purposes may be.

Nevertheless, people are people. If you are really interested in magic, chances are you're going to give this a try. I'm not saying you should, and I'm not saying you shouldn't. I'm saying that it would be wise to remember that you may get side effects that you didn't want and didn't foresee, and may not be entirely pleasant.

Any use of power comes with certain dangers. These powers are potentially far greater than those in nuclear reactors because they come much closer to the fundamental forces of the universe. We as humans have access to these forces, although for the most part we aren't aware of them and don't have the discipline to use them. If you train yourself to use these powers, make sure to do so responsibly, ethically, and with human decency at the forefront.

8

Thought Power

Thought power has become incredibly popular in America. I'll give you a little bit of its history. In the nineteenth century, certain healers realized that the mind could affect healing as much as or more than physical remedies. This isn't too surprising, because given the quality of medicine at that time, the physical remedies were at least as likely to do harm as good.

Even so, the mind has some role in healing. This was understood first by a man named Phineas Quimby, who was a healer in Maine around the time of the Civil War. His pupil Mary Baker Eddy was the founder of Christian Science, which is all about this type of healing.

There were many others who used the principles of mind healing, which became known as New Thought. By the end of the nineteenth century, it had become very popular.

In the early twentieth century, people started to think, "If we can use this mind power for healing, why can't we use it for success and prosperity?" So a whole cornucopia of books, tapes, and audios came out preaching thought power for success. Many of them say that if you visualize riches, they will come on their own.

Why? I've already explained why: if you hold a mental picture and invest it with enough energy, it will, so the theory goes, manifest in the physical world. Success books often teach that you should visualize the desired object as concretely as you can. You imagine it with all of the senses: you're sitting in your dream car, riding around in it, feeling happy as a millionaire. You feel it, you experience it, and eventually it will come to pass, often in ways that you didn't expect.

This is the use of thought power. Many people have succeeded using methods like this (although the most powerful versions emphasize that you need to take concrete, positive action as well). But again, it is very hard to have this process work without some undesired consequences. You need $100,000. Your uncle drops dead and leaves you $100,000. Did you want your uncle to drop dead? No, you probably didn't, but the Force, with its light side and dark side, is really quite amoral. You got what you wanted, but you lost your uncle. Well, that's too bad. I say this having had similar experiences and having made similar mistakes.

One way of preventing negative consequences is to use the proviso, stated in archaic language, "An it harm none," meaning, if it doesn't harm anybody. That can work, but even so the results rarely if ever turn out exactly as we might have hoped.

I've often likened this kind of magic to sculpting nitroglycerin. Nitroglycerin is a very sloppy, jellylike substance. It's also very explosive. Playing with the astral light is much like that. You are sculpting something that may even be more explosive, with far more repercussions than you might imagine.

Let's turn to positive thinking and affirmation. Despite the nonsense written about these things, the core concept has a great deal of truth. If you have a positive mindset, you are more likely to have positive consequences in your life.

Why? Next time you go to the store, imagine that everybody there is your enemy and is there to thwart you, the salespeople are no good, and you hate the place; they never have what you want anyway. See what kind of experience you have.

Later, go to the same store. Tell yourself, "This is a great store. I love this place. I always have a wonderful time here. I always get what I want. The salespeople are so nice. The people are so nice." See what kind of experience you get out of this. I think you will find that the second experience will be more pleasant.

Yet negative expectations pervade our lives. They pollute the mental air as auto exhaust pollutes the physical air. If the astral light, the psyche, is like a sea, you could think of these thoughts as sea creatures. Some of them are benign, but there are a lot of bad ones floating around out there.

We've always heard that we're all connected; we're all one. Although I will talk about this more in a later chapter, it partly means that other people's thoughts are swimming around in the same ocean that your thoughts are swimming in. If you turn down the volume on your own negative thoughts, you will not necessarily get rid of others' harmful thoughts, but at least you are not contributing your own.

As you look more into your mind, you may find that a lot of your thoughts are negative. You expect politicians to be crooks. You expect the world to be awful. You expect the worst possible things to happen. This situation is not accidental, because the media are all about bad news, rarely showing good news.

Given that you can't stop this process on a large scale, what do you do? You can't move to a mountaintop. Or maybe you can, but what good will it do? You are still living in the same psychic sea as everyone else. The best way to insulate yourself from negative thoughts is to have positive thoughts. A simple one, which has worked for many people, is to say, "I like myself." In reality, I may not like myself in all ways or at all times. But as a positive affirmation, it can be quite helpful.

Affirmation can be much more elaborate. One of the most important spiritual texts of the twentieth century is *A Course in Miracles.* This is a channeled work, meaning that Helen Schucman, the woman who wrote it, didn't think she was writing it; she believed she was receiving dictation from an unseen source. (I discuss the Course at length in my book *A Theology of Love.*) The Course is extremely powerful. It contains 365 daily lessons, many of which are powerful affirmations. Here's one: *I am not the victim of the world I see.*

Think about it. There is an underlying assumption that as far as the universe is concerned, you are a dead sea slug lying on the beach for the ants to eat. That's not the case at all. If you think that way, you can weaken yourself, but it's still not the case. You're really quite free.

At the very least, look at all of the negative thought forms that are floating out there. Other people have them. The media have them. Wherever you come across them, realize, "I'm not the victim of these thoughts. I can be quite free of them. They have nothing to do with me." That is a major step toward inner freedom.

9

Prophecy

There are two kinds of forecasters: those who don't know and those who don't know they don't know.

—JOHN KENNETH GALBRAITH

Our relation to the future is rather funny. We are able to foresee the future to some extent. You have some idea of your weekend plans or what you'll be doing tonight at 9:00 p.m. You may even have ideas about your career or life goals.

As humans, we can foresee the future, but we can't foresee it all that well. We see it only in little bits and chunks. Unexpected things inevitably happen. This leads to a dilemma about predicting the future.

Futurologists—experts who draw up forecasts for think tanks and governments—have only one thing to go on: past trends. If past trends continue, we will be at a certain point in 2050.

Unfortunately, current trends never continue. There are always dislocations, upheavals, freak events that derail expectations. War, disease, stock market crashes—which sometimes seem to be explicable, sometimes not—disrupt the foreseen future. An honest futurologist will simply say, "This is what I can say given the information I have."

Another kind of person who attempts to predict the future is the prophet, the one who has visions, dreams, revelations about things to come. This individual is in exactly the opposite position, because dislocations, pestilences, wars, cataclysms, fire from above, are his stock-in-trade. If he predicted the future by saying, "I don't see too much happening down the line. I think everything's going to seem pretty normal," he would not get much attention.

Those are the two dilemmas in predicting the future: we have to go by current trends, or we can count on disruptions, except nobody knows what these will be. Whenever we are looking ahead to the future, we have to keep these limitations in mind.

I myself do not believe in prophecy. Practically all of the prophecies I have encountered have simply been wrong. This includes many of those in the Bible. Here's one example: certain sections of the synoptic Gospels predict the future (they can be found in Matthew 24, Mark 13, and Luke 21). They are similar and come from a common source, so scholars refer to them collectively as the Apocalyptic Discourse or the Little Apocalypse.

If you take these prophecies at face value, Jesus appears to be predicting that the Romans will invade Judea and destroy the Temple in Jerusalem. This part came true. In AD 70, the Romans destroyed Jerusalem and sacked the Temple, and it was never rebuilt. It has never been rebuilt to this day.

But if you read on, this discourse sounds very much as if the sack of Jerusalem is a prelude to the end of the world. Up to a point, this looks like a prophecy that came true, but beyond a certain point, it doesn't look so good. The world did not come to an end. It still has not come to an end almost two thousand years later.

Admittedly, New Testament scholarship is an incredibly complicated subject. The most serious and respected scholars have had to admit that it's impossible to determine precisely what Jesus Christ said and what was put in his mouth afterward. Very likely he made at least some or most of these statements, but which ones? In addition, many of these utterances were almost certainly delivered at different times and were stitched together well after Jesus's lifetime. This means that the context of these statements is completely missing. Jesus could have been predicting the Roman invasion at one time and the end of the world at another.

Nevertheless, this prophecy, as it has come down to us, simply didn't come true. (For more discussion of this issue, see my book *How God Became God: What Scholars Are Really Saying about God and the Bible*.)

I'll give you another example. Several years ago, I wrote a book on Nostradamus, the famed French prophet of the sixteenth century. Nostradamus was, in his way, a brilliant poet. He wrote quatrains, four-line verses, that are jagged, disrupted, and obscure. Had he lived in the twentieth century, he would probably have been regarded as a brilliant surrealist poet. The prophecies in these verses can be interpreted to mean any number of things. But insofar as I was able to pin any of them down to specific meanings, practically none came true.

I'll even tell you about the most famous prophecy, which supposedly came true, except maybe it didn't, because he wasn't predicting what he was thought to predict. I'll quote this quatrain in full, in my translation from my book *The Essential Nostradamus*:

Forty-five degrees, the sky will burn,
Fire to approach the great new city.
Instantly a great scattered flame will leap up,
When one wants to make proof of the Normans.

(*Prophecies*, 6.97)

Many people have said that Nostradamus is talking about New York—the "new city." But he probably wasn't, because Nostradamus didn't even say that his prophecies had anything to do with the Americas. What, then, did he mean?

The name of the city of Naples in southern Italy comes from the Greek *Neapolis* (the city was founded in ancient times by the Greeks). Naples is only nine miles from a volcano called Vesuvius, which erupted in AD 79 and destroyed the Roman cities of Pompeii and Herculaneum. What, then, was Nostradamus's prophecy? In all likelihood, that Naples would be destroyed by a volcano. Up to this point, this hasn't happened either.

In short, few of these prophecies have ever come true, and not in any form that would have been at all useful. As a result, prophecies of the Last Days, the apocalypse, the millennium all need to be taken them with an enormous grain of salt.

I am not saying that the future is always impossible to glimpse, but most prophecies haven't come true, even those of the Bible. Generally, the more grandiose, the more fantastic, the more pretentious the prophecy, the more likely it is to be false.

Some prophecies have a better record. The ones that have struck me the most have been those made by indigenous elders about what they call *earth changes*: predictions of great disturbances in the natural world in the near future. Made decades ago, they are starting to look as if they're coming true with climate change and other environmental upheavals.

How did the elders know these things? What did they see? Possibly they were more in tune with natural processes and phenomena than we Westerners are; therefore they may have seen certain signs in the natural world that signaled the coming of grim and disastrous events. They may have been able to see these trends not only before you and me, but even before meteorologists and climatologists.

If what I've said is true, why then, is there such obsession with the end times? Partly from Christianity, because Christianity had these expectations from the beginning, as we've seen. But I think the apocalyptic obsession has to do with issues that touch us much more deeply.

Here is a little fact that you and I both know infallibly: your world is going to end in a few decades. So is mine. So is everyone else's. Our world is going to end, because we are going to die. This is perhaps the most naked, obvious, and irrefutable truth about human existence. It is, however, uncomfortable to think about.

Psychologists talk about *displacement*. That is to say, you're afraid of something. You're so afraid of it that you don't even want to look at it. All the same, you're aware of it at some level, and it causes you discomfort. You deal with this discomfort by displacing your fear onto something else.

I believe that fears about the end times and the Last Days are displacements of our own fears of death. We also afraid to face another fact: we usually die alone. Even if we're surrounded by grieving loved ones, we still die alone, because they're not coming with us, at least not now. In certain respects, this possibility is as terrifying as death itself. Thus the idea that everyone is going to perish or come to judgment at the same time may, perversely, be reassuring to some people.

There is a deep need to avoid an irrefutable truth—our own death—and project it onto something that is very likely not going to happen. If the world ends, it's not going to be because Jesus is appearing in the skies above Dallas and cars are going to be crashing because their drivers have been raptured. The world is not going to end that way, if only because God is not the creator of a B-grade movie.

If you take some of these things into consideration, I believe that you'll be freed from a lot of irrational fears and come a little bit closer to your own situation, because you are going to die. It is even a spiritual practice to contemplate the fact of your own death.

The good news is, the world is unlikely to end anytime soon. The bad news is, *your* world is going to end. So is mine. These are the facts of life.

10

Psychic Powers

Is the future, then, totally unforeseeable? Not entirely, although I believe that if we do see anything accurate about the future, we're going to see it patchily.

In that case, why should we be able to see anything at all? The answer is grounded in some of the ideas we've already discussed.

Remember thought forms? The idea is that to make something happen in reality, you create a thought form first. Suppose that this is true not only for our intentions but for all events. They would have to appear in the astral world before manifesting in palpable reality.

Theoretically, then, if you have some view of this astral world, you may glimpse what is coming to pass. But making contact with the astral realm consciously and deliberately is problematic. Some people appear to do it, but even most of them do so spottily. The psychic Jeane Dixon became famous in the sixties for predicting that John F. Kennedy would be assassinated, but her track record as a whole was not as impressive: she also predicted, for example, that Russia would be the first country to land on the moon.

At certain times, you do get premonitions and foreshadowings. Usually they are not visual: you don't necessarily have a mental image of what's going to happen. More often these premonitions are more sensory, a felt feeling, or sometimes an audial message that you hear inside your head: "Something told me not to take that plane. Something told me not to get involved with that person." These intuitions can be vague and inarticulate, but they are not to be dismissed out of hand.

This takes us back to the issue of connecting various parts of oneself. Usually in our culture, the more emotional, intuitive side is cut off from the mental side; it's not given its due. When in doubt, we usually give the victory to the head. If we don't have a rational objection to taking a certain step, we usually go ahead, even if we have an irrational objection to it.

This approach is obviously a mistake, because you're not using all of the information provided by your own cognition. Part of you says something is a good idea; part of you has a bad feeling about it. Which is right? Neither one is always right. If you can step back, look at input from both of these sources, take them as parts of a whole—as pieces of information that you work with—and make your decision from there, you'll probably be much better off. You'll trust your intuition up to a point, but it's never a good idea to be the slave of anything, even your own intuition.

In this sense, it may be possible to have psychic powers, at least at certain times, and thus foresee the future. Such things have occurred in many instances. But you are far more likely to have such glimpses of future events insofar as they concern you personally. Your intuitions about larger events—elections, say—are usually too heavily conditioned by your preconceptions and preferences to be of much value.

Incidentally, an enormous amount of research has been done on psychic powers over the last eighty years in the most respected universities. Taken as a whole, these findings lead to this conclusion: yes, there is some capacity for psi (psychic powers such as precognition, clairvoyance, and psychokinesis) in humans. As a whole, people guess correctly on card guessing tests more than they should statistically should, but only a little. People have a little bit of psychic ability, although in most of us is extremely weak.

That is what scientific findings are saying. If someone says, "Science has proved all this stuff is a load of bunk," they're wrong. Science has done no such thing. These psi experiments are very likely more rigorous and more thoroughly documented than those for the prescription medication you are taking now.

There is such a thing as psi, and you possess it to some degree. How do you get in touch with it? One of the most important indications is one that I've already given: it has to do with a felt sense. *Clairvoyance* has many meanings, but sometimes it refers to the ability to see the psychic field around another person. Clairvoyants see certain colors around people: muddy, dense colors generally represent negative thought forms; bright, intense colors indicate positive ones. A good clairvoyant can make specific and accurate predictions and diagnoses on the basis of what she sees.

I know people who have clairvoyant powers. Usually they were born with them. Many have improved their abilities with training and practice, but it's like being a great pianist: even though you need plenty of training, you're going to go a lot farther if you have the innate talent.

Clairvoyants are rare exceptions. They're fascinating people, and their insights are often remarkable, but most of us aren't like that.

How, then, do we get in touch with these powers? As I've already suggested, part of the answer has to do with gut feelings. That is to say, we perceive a lot of things that are not grasped by the five known senses, but we do not see them clairvoyantly; rather, we experience them viscerally. A sense of feeling right or feeling wrong is a very important part of intuition. To use somewhat technical language, our psychic powers are kinesthetic: we have access to them through our feelings rather than seeing or hearing.

The most productive way of cultivating paranormal powers, then, is to be aware of these feelings. If something tells you not to go into a place, it doesn't always mean you should run away, but you should take note of your impressions. If you go in anyway, see what happens. Sometimes nothing. Sometimes you realize what a huge mistake it was.

This sense that I'm talking about is not infallible, but often it's right. It's probably more right than wrong. People generally disregard it to their own detriment.

You can go far with this investigation. The most important thing is awareness of what's going on in yourself. People who are introspective or introverted usually find this easier to do than others. Nevertheless, to some degree, developing this ability is probably useful for everyone.

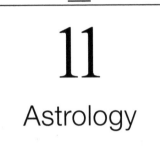

11

Astrology

I n the past two chapters, we've been talking about various approaches to knowing the future. Let me go on to one of the most universal methods: astrology.

What is the difference between astronomy and astrology? As I see it, astronomy is the study of the stars, the galaxies, space, and planets, as they are in themselves rather than in relation to us. Astrology, on the other hand, is about cosmic celestial events as they relate to human life. Do the stars have an influence on us? From a lot of different angles, it looks as if they do.

You're probably familiar with astrology at least to the degree of knowing what your sun sign is. That is not a complete astrological picture. There's a lot more to it. The sun sign says something about who you are in essence, but many other factors, including astrological ones, influence how you manifest this essence to the outside world.

Typically, astrologers will focus on several things: the planets, something called the ascendant, and their relation to each other and their place in your astrological chart. Your chart is based on the place, the date, and the time you were born—the exact minute if at all possible, because even an hour or so can change things quite a bit.

Of course, not everyone knows their birth time, and the astrologer has to work with what she's given: "I think my mother said I was born in the morning." But the more precisely you know this information, the more accurate your astrological reading is likely to be.

Astrologically, the most important planets are the sun, the moon, Mercury, Venus, Mars, Jupiter, and Saturn. (We know that the sun and moon are astronomically not planets, but they are taken as such in astrology.) The outer planets, Neptune, Uranus, and Pluto, also figure into the picture, but for the sake of this short discussion, I'm going to stay with the seven visible planets.

Astrologers relate the planets to certain qualities. The sun is your essence, the way you really are. The moon has more to do with your personality. Venus relates to love, sex, reproduction. Mars governs aggression, assertiveness, anger. Jupiter deals with religion, philosophy, magnanimity, philanthropy. Saturn has to do with discipline, the hard lessons of life.

All of these planets have some relation to one another in your chart. Certain relations are harmonious, that is, the energies flow well. If Venus and Mars, for example, are in harmony, your assertive side and your more passive, feminine side (as well as your sex drive) work well together. If the aspects (as these planetary relations are called) are not good, these areas in your life may prove to be difficult. If your sun and your moon are in conflict, the way you are could very well be at odds with the way you seem.

Astrology can produce some striking insights. One of my oldest and closest friends is extremely brilliant, possibly a genius, but he's also extremely eccentric. I happened to have his astrological chart. I have another friend who's one of the most prominent and respected astrologers in the country, and I was meeting him for drinks. I was curious about my eccentric friend's chart and brought it along. The astrologer looked at it for five seconds and said, "Wow. That's a difficult childhood." The friend whose chart this was had the worst childhood of anyone I've ever known. How could the astrologer see that? We were at a brew pub, and he had glanced at the chart for about five seconds. That's what you can do if you know astrology extremely well.

Although I'm not a professional astrologer, I know the basics, and sometimes I can see certain things through astrology. When George W. Bush was inaugurated, I decided to cast a chart for his administration: January 20, 2001, Washington, D.C., 12:06 p.m. (I had checked my watch for the exact moment he was sworn in). When I did, I looked at the chart and said, "Wow! It looks like we're going to have a war!" (Mars, which governs war, was badly aspected.) But the nation was at peace at the time. I thought, "That's ridiculous. Whom are we going to have a war with?" Events showed soon enough.

How, then, does astrology work? As I've pointed out, the astral light is the world of forms, of dreams, images, thoughts. It has its name because it has long been believed to be closely connected with the planets: therefore seeing the position of the planets give you a sense of what is going on in the world of forms, and what might or might not happen in the actual world.

It is not a good idea to be superstitious about astrology or to think, "The astrology is bad today, so I'm going to hide under my bed." Astrology does have some accuracy; it can tell you a lot about you; it can tell you something about what may be ahead for you. Not, however, in a deterministic way. It would be unwise to say, "A terrible thing is going to happen to you on this date." The old astrologers did that, but we've gone away from this practice. You can look at astrology and astrological readings as a weather report: I can see the sort of thing that's coming; I don't know what exactly it's going to be.

During 2019, the astrological world was abuzz over a conjunction of Pluto and Saturn, two planets with dark, heavy energy, that was due to be exact on January 12, 2020. One astrology website, Astrology.com, says about this aspect: the planets' "proximity constellates a period of intensified tension, constraint, and division in collective events ... societal structures decay and breakdown [sic]." This date closely coincides with the coming of the coronavirus (especially since the motions of these planets is so slow that this aspect takes place over several months), which has produced some of the greatest dislocations of recent decades. Astrologers foresaw a great upheaval coming, although they could not specifically say what it would be.

Can astrology be used for romantic compatibility? I would say yes. Compatible sun signs give a greater chance for romantic success and stability. (I won't go into the specifics of these affinities, because they are discussed in any number of books and websites.) The great psychiatrist C. G. Jung noted that there were certain aspects that were more promising for marriage. (If you want to read more about this, it's in his book *Synchronicity: An Acausal Connecting Principle.*) He started with traditional astrological principles, examined the charts of several hundred married couples, and he found that statistically, the astrological affinities did work out.

There is, then, some basis for taking astrology seriously. But as with intuition or indeed anything else, it is not wise to be deterministic, superstitious, or fatalistic about it. Astrology is, like many of the other things I've been discussing in this book, a form of information that you can fit into the greater whole of your conceptual reality.

This thought goes back to a theme I was talking about at the beginning of this book: our connection to something greater. By the materialistic view, we have no such connection; we're just a bunch of bugs crawling around a ball of dirt. This view is unsatisfying, and I would say it's unsatisfying because it's untrue. Astrology is one way of showing how we are connected to a larger whole. In that respect at least, I believe it has a great deal to offer.

12

The Tarot

In this chapter, I want to turn to the Tarot, which is a deck of cards commonly used to predict the future.

There are many misconceptions about the Tarot. Sometimes you will hear that it is Satanic, which it is not; it has nothing to do with Satanism. There's a lot of other lore about the Tarot that's not quite so pernicious but is also untrue. Rather than debunking all these beliefs, let me tell you the facts about the Tarot. Of course I will have to leave out many important details.

The Tarot is a deck of seventy-eight cards. Fifty-six of these are very much like playing cards, which have fifty-two cards in a deck, four suits, with three court cards in each suit. The Tarot deck has a fourth court card called the knight—king, queen, knight, page (the equivalent of the jack in the regular cards)—for a total of fifty-six.

Then there are twenty-two other cards, which are called trumps. The name of these cards reveal the origins of the Tarot, which was invented in northern Italy around 1450. These trump cards show many strange figures, such as the Chariot, Death, the Emperor, the Hermit, the Hanged Man, the Sun, and the World. Where do they come from?

In Italy at that time, there were parades called *trionfi* or triumphs. These parades would have carts rather like our present-day floats, which were decorated to show certain allegorical figures. There is a famous cycle of poems by the fourteenth-century Italian poet Petrarch called *Trionfi*. In it death triumphs over love, but fame triumphs over death, and so on.

This idea was turned into a card game. The Tarot was originally a specialized card game deck. Dozens of games have been documented that you can play with these cards, although they are more popular on the European continent than in the English-speaking countries.

In the 1700s, the French scholar Antoine Court de Gébelin wrote a treatise saying that the Tarot cards, especially the twenty-two trumps, contained the codified knowledge of ancient Egypt. This set the educated world into a furor. Suddenly, everyone was interested in knowing what these secret truths were.

I am not going to say that Court de Gébelin's claim was either true or false. I will say that discussing and exploring the history of the Tarot would take a great deal of time and a great deal of speculation. Here I would prefer to go on and simply say that the images of the Tarot, particularly the twenty-two trumps, speak to us at a deep symbolic level.

In the twentieth century, C. G. Jung came up with the highly influential theory of the archetypes of the collective unconscious. By Jung's view, these are structures that are built into our minds—that in a sense constitute our minds. By calling it the collective unconscious, Jung meant that this part of the mind is common to the whole human race (which is not surprising, given that our minds are so similar). These structures, said Jung, were the building blocks of the human psyche. They were reflected in mythic figures and stories that appear worldwide, as well as in the dreams of ordinary people.

Archetypes include figures like the Great Mother, the Trickster, and the Wise Old Man. Jung and his followers have shown that these figures occur practically universally, in all myths at all times. One of the most famous authors to expound on this theme was the mythologist Joseph Campbell.

What do the archetypes have to do with the Tarot? Quite simply, those twenty-two trumps, sometimes called the Major Arcana, are a kind of catalogue of Jung's archetypes, each of which can fit into one or more of those Tarot cards. The Trickster, for example, could be correlated to the Magician of the Tarot; the Wise Old Man is very much like the Hermit card.

These figures exist in the structures of our minds. There is within you a trickster. There is within you a wise old man. If you see these sides of yourself, the all-important goal of self-knowledge comes a little bit closer. Sometimes a person lives out one of these archetypes in an obvious way, like the woman who becomes the big mama, the overflowing abundant mother, whether she has children or not. The warrior who wants to fight for the right is symbolized in the Tarot trump called the Chariot. There's also the Devil. There are angels as well.

This is, I think, what the Tarot is fundamentally about. Study and reflection upon these images are ways of gaining access to the deeper levels of our own minds.

The Tarot is also used for one of many methods of divination. (You can do the same thing with ordinary playing cards.) Another method, which even more ancient than the Tarot, is the Chinese oracle the *I Ching*, the Book of Changes. In this process, you either throw coins or you draw from piles of sticks and create a six-lined figure that correlates to one of sixty-four images in the *I Ching*. This hexagram highlights your situation. It may show you something that you may not have seen or known about a given situation, as well as a direction for action.

These processes all rely upon controlled randomness. There are seventy-eight Tarot cards and sixty-four hexagrams, any of which could appear in a given reading. They gauge patterns in the astral world, which may presage happenings on earth.

Again, this process is not deterministic. Indications point in a certain direction: they are not sentences of doom. Divination, at its best, is meant to give general guidance for action rather than announcing what an ironclad fate is going to drop on your head. That's because you do have free will; you have freedom of choice. These methods reveal some options that may be more likely to happen, but not what inevitably will happen.

There is another form of divination, in which a person goes into a light trance and gazes at some surface. The crystal ball is the most famous example. If you gaze at it in a relaxed, almost sleepy, drowsy state, certain images will come, which may tell you about the future. You can divine (the verb form of *divination*) with something as simple as a bowl of water. Some people gaze into their thumbnails. There was a famous magus in the sixteenth century named John Dee, who used a black obsidian tablet that had been taken from the Aztecs. For a long time, it was on permanent display at the Ashmolean Museum at the University of Oxford.

You can use all sorts of things in order to gaze a little more deeply into the astral realm, where there are forms whose swirlings may show what's about to manifest. Used in a way that is humble, practical, and respectful, particularly of your own and other's free will, I think these forms of divination can be useful and illuminating.

13

Ghosts, Angels, and Spirits

Let's turn our attention now to life forms that are usually invisible to us: ghosts, spirits, and angels. To return to my metaphor of the ocean of being, the world of thoughts, images, feelings—what I've called the astral realm—are like an ocean as well. It's inhabited by a great number of creatures, some of which may look beautiful to us, some of which seem repellent.

In talking about inhabitants of the unseen world, it's a good idea to keep this analogy in mind. As you know if you watch nature shows, there are creatures in the ocean that are revoltingly ugly but are quite harmless.

Just because something is ugly doesn't necessarily mean it's evil. The same is true in the alternate realms.

As a prelude, I want to talk a little bit about science. Over the last two hundred years, the scientific world-view has been somewhat dishonest. It has not always highlighted the fact that its findings are always provisional and subject to later refutation. Indeed this is the core of the scientific method. One famous philosopher of science, Karl Popper, said that if you reach any definite conclusions in science, you've given up the game. Nevertheless, science has often permitted us to believe that what it tells us about the universe is the truth.

Yet science relies on empirical data, which are ultimately sense data, and our senses are very limited. We can only see a very narrow band of the electromagnetic spectrum; we can hear another small band. There's a great deal that we can't see or hear. We have enhanced our senses with microscopes, telescopes, and other instruments, but they have only increased the bandwidth somewhat. In short, what we find through all of these instruments is still only an extremely narrow band of what is actually out there.

Science has had to come to a conclusion like this one. Scientists have reason to believe that most of the energy and matter in the universe are not directly perceptible by us or by our instruments. They are called *dark matter* and *dark energy*. The NASA Science website tells us,

"Roughly 68% of the universe is dark energy. Dark matter makes up about 27%. The rest—everything on Earth, everything ever observed with all of our instruments, all normal matter—adds up to less than 5% of the universe."

How science has made such determinations is a subject beyond my scope. Nevertheless, you can't accept these facts and then try to pretend that what you're seeing in your own little spectrum of the senses is the whole story about reality. Those are two mutually inconsistent claims. This is a great problem for the scientific worldview, and it will force science to change radically, as it is already doing. I am neither a scientist nor a philosopher of science, so I'm not going to take the argument any further.

We have some reason to believe that there are many things in the universe that are real, although we don't perceive them with our ordinary senses, and that these things may affect us.

"That's ridiculous," you might say. But five hundred years ago, people had no idea of bacteria or viruses, even though these microscopic creatures caused all sorts of terrible effects. In the fourteenth century, the Black Death wiped out a quarter of the population of Europe. No one knew that it was caused by bacteria, because the existence of bacteria was unknown at the time.

We may be affected by many things that our current senses can't pick up. This idea can be either frightening or reassuring, depending on whether you think the universe is fundamentally good, fundamentally evil, or some combination of the two (a subject I will return to).

In any event, there are very likely many beings that we don't perceive with our ordinary senses. These may be what we have called ghost, spirits, angels, and devils. No doubt there's as wide a variety of them as there are creatures and species in the natural world. There is a good deal of lore about these entities. Some of it is superstition, but some of it may be based on perceptions of reality.

To take the argument one step further, there may be—very likely are—entities that we do not normally see but that can still affect and interact with us, at least at times.

Let me begin with the good side. One almost universal theme in human life is the belief that there are good beings who help us. These are unseen, invisible helpers, common called angels. The Catholic church teaches that everybody has a guardian angel. This may or may not be so, but in all likelihood there are beings in other realms that can help us if we ask for their help. This may be why people have a powerful impulse toward prayer whenever they're in any extreme situation, because we know that often enough, you can get help of some mysterious kind if you call upon it.

There's a famous story about the Battle of Mons in 1914 in World War I. Arthur Machen, a British fiction writer, wrote a story which said that angels were helping the British troops at this battle. It was fiction, but a very peculiar thing happened. Men from the front wrote to the magazine that published this story and said, "That did happen. I did actually see that." Some have even said that St. George, the patron saint of England, was fighting. To be frank, the British army didn't too well in that battle (it ended up retreating 250 miles), but maybe it could have done even worse.

Some cultures identify these beings with the ancestors, who can help us, particularly if we honor them; if we don't, sometimes they can be peevish. There are cults of ancestor worship in many cultures and civilizations, including China.

In some cases, people find that a recently deceased grandparent or parent shows up to help them at a critical moment. These stories are difficult to take completely at face value, but it would be equally foolish, in my opinion, to dismiss them entirely. Too many people have had these experiences in too many different places and reported very similar things to justify total skepticism.

Here's another little-known fact: it is said that the human being has a capacity to create in exactly the way God creates. This is a very obscure point, but it does have some ramifications here. In the Jewish mystical tradition known as the Kabbalah, it is said that every good deed, *mitzvah* in the Hebrew, creates an angel, so you may be creating actual beings by your thoughts and actions—a thought that should give us an enormous sense of responsibility.

On the spiritual path, responsibility is an extremely important theme. You have to be much more aware of yourself and the possible consequences of your actions, both good and bad, and behave accordingly. You can feel the vibes that people are emanating, and you have responsibility for the vibes you're emanating.

Most people know when a room has a good feeling about it. They don't know why, because superficially the room looks very much like any other, but it will have a certain palpable atmosphere. People tend to agree about whether a particular place feels creepy or benign. If spiritual or religious rites have been carried out for a long time in a given room, it may have an aura of sanctity. Many people feel this in the great cathedrals of Europe.

In short, there are, at least potentially, beings who can help us and can work with us. Sometimes they may be or look like deceased relatives (I'll talk about life after death in the next chapter). I think beliefs in these beings are worth taking seriously. I wouldn't suggest that you drive recklessly in the hope that some angel will pull you out of it at the last minute (although that does happen and has happened; many people feel they owe their lives to it). If you are open to it, there is help from the other side. In all likelihood, we are not alone, and many of the beings we can't see are beneficent and take an interest us.

14

Life after Death

At this point I want to talk about the spirits of deceased human beings. No doubt there are many beings in the other worlds that have never been human beings, never will be human beings, and have no resemblance to human beings. But deceased humans seem to be part of the picture. As a matter of fact, it is quite common to experience the presence of a deceased loved one, particularly in the first few days after death.

Years ago I edited a magazine on mysticism called *Gnosis* (from a Greek word meaning *knowledge*). We got sheaves of first-person accounts, totally unsolicited, of supernatural experiences, particularly seeing dead relatives. We almost never published these articles; I usually sent them back with a polite note.

Why were people sending these pieces to us? Obviously they'd had these experiences, were fascinated or disturbed by them, and probably did not know anybody who would even believe them. No doubt they would get answers like, "You were just imaging things" or "It was just a dream."

Sadly for American religion, many people have gone to their ministers and priests with these experiences and gotten nothing like a satisfactory answer. Yet these are trained professionals who are supposed to have some knowledge of the supernatural and help us mediate our experiences with it. This regrettable fact explains a great deal about our civilization and culture today.

In any event, it does appear that the presence of the deceased stays in the vicinity for a brief time after death. Here is one theory that comes out of the influential mystical tradition known as Theosophy. As I said in an earlier chapter, at death the life force leaves the body. The idea is that you have an energetic body, which consists of this life force. It underlies the physical body and keeps it going; the Theosophists call this the *etheric double* or *etheric body*. At the moment of death, this etheric body is severed from the physical body. A biblical verse is believed to allude to this fact: "Or ever the silver cord be loosed, or the golden bowl be broken, or the pitcher be broken at the fountain, or the wheel be broken at the cistern. Then shall the dust return to the earth as it was: and the spirit shall return unto God who gave it" (Ecclesiastes 12:6–7). The "silver cord" may refer to the bond between the physical and the etheric bodies.

The etheric body survives the physical body for a short while (the traditional time is three days, although no doubt there is some variation) and hangs around the vicinity.

In the last chapter, I mentioned the angels at the Battle of Mons. Some have speculated that the forms that the soldiers saw were not angels but the etheric bodies of dead soldiers. They were still present and were not even aware they were dead, so they continued fighting.

In the astral world, the world of thoughts, forms, and ideas, we also have a kind of body, which has been called the *astral body*. This body lasts a little longer than the etheric body. The amount of time traditionally given for the survival of the astral body is forty days, so some religious traditions will have a service forty days after the person's death.

A famous and powerful text called the *Tibetan Book of the Dead* is so called because it contains instructions for the recently deceased. A lama reads this book aloud to the dying person and continues to read it after the person's death. The text gives precise instructions about what to do in the different realms of the afterlife. The idea is to guide the person through the death of the etheric body and the astral body. Tibetans read this text to the deceased person for forty-nine days after death.

After this point, this astral body dies too, which may be a bit disturbing because it involves the death of the personality. Your personality is going to die after you do, probably a little later than your physical body does. That is a sobering fact, because most people identify almost completely with their personalities, yet these personalities are going to die, just like the body. Nevertheless, it is clearly the case, as we can see from the obvious fact that the personality is chiefly concerned with earthly concerns. Are you going to be a Republican or a Democrat after you're dead? Why would you possibly care? Are you going to still like ice cream? You won't have anything to eat it with.

The harsh truth is that many of the things you think you are are going to die. This is one reason death is so frightening. You think you're your body. Well, your body is going to die; you know that. Your personality is going to last maybe a little bit longer. If you think you consist entirely of those two things, it seems hopeless.

People wonder who they really are, because they intuitively know they are not their bodies or personalities but have no idea of what else there might be. Hence you don't know what is really you, and what you think is you is not really you; it's just a vehicle that you're temporarily using to experience life in a certain form.

It's not hopeless. There is a part of you that survives. It can be called the Self, the true "I." The Self, this "I," can never be lost. It's indestructible—the "something eternal" mentioned by Thornton Wilder.

The goal is not to identify with the destructible, but with the indestructible. The Hindus know this. A Hindu prayer, which comes from an ancient scripture called the Upanishads, says, "Lead us from the unreal to the real." In part that means, lead us from identifying with the body, with the personality, to realizing that we are the true "I."

I will go more into this subject later, but for now, let's go back to discussing ghosts and spirits. The process of death doesn't always go as it should. The etheric body and the astral body are *supposed* to die: this is the natural course of things. In a way, it is a mercy. Richard Smoley is a decent and in some ways remarkable fellow, but the idea of being Richard Smoley for eternity does not appeal to me.

Under certain circumstances, it sometimes happens that this astral body, this complex of thoughts, energies, and emotions that constitute the personality, is kept alive through some energetic connection with the physical world. This is sometimes called the *astral shell*, and it may be responsible for some hauntings and even for certain types of spirit possession. In these cases, something has going wrong; some bit of energy didn't die that was supposed to die, and it has fixed onto a susceptible living person and lives by sucking its vital force.

This idea would explain the origin of beliefs about vampirism. The vampire of the movies, the bloodsucker, is familiar to everyone. Similarly, certain astral entities can attach themselves to living people and suck the life force out of them (rather than blood as such). There may, then, be something to the concept of vampirism, although it's not likely to resemble the cartoonish Hollywood version.

These astral shells are not necessarily evil, even if they may be somewhat predatory. Ultimately, they're just lost souls. Like the soldiers at Mons, they may not even know they're dead. Specialists who work with entities like this tell them, "You're stuck at a level where you shouldn't be, and it's time to move on. Go into the light." There are people who can and do work this way, apparently with good results.

These considerations, I think, go far toward explaining many paranormal phenomena. These entities may well exist, but there is no reason to fear them, because they are far less powerful than you. You can usually get rid of them quite easily. Occasionally I have felt some sort of spirit attack during sleep. Initially these encounters were frightening, but after once or twice, I got the hang of driving them away without much effort. In a sense, these things are easier to get rid of than mosquitoes, because you can usually just tell them to shove off, whereas with the mosquito, you have to take the trouble of getting up, turning on the light, finding the mosquito, and killing it.

Paranormal entities are a part of the natural world, although a far vaster natural world than we customarily imagine. We can deal with these beings as they may come up. The power remains ours. You have far more power than any entity you will encounter. Your greatest protection is to remember that.

15

Evil

Once a man and woman came to God and said, "Hey, Lord, we've heard there's this thing called good and evil. It sounds cool, and we'd like to see what it's like."

"That is not a good idea," said God. "I do not suggest you do this."

"Oh, come on. We want to."

"All right," said God. "You can have your way, but you're going to have to go down into a realm where it hurts to have babies, and you have to work hard to earn your living."

I've just retold the story of the Garden of Eden in a colloquial fashion. Viewed this way, the myth of the Fall in Genesis is not just a story but a profound statement of the human condition.

The universal human, who is both male and female, is all of us. We are all parts of that primordial being who wished to know good and evil. Created to live in the astral world, it figuratively fell down to earth, broke into little pieces, and became individuals such as you and me.

I have no idea of who you are. In all likelihood, I will never meet you. But I can make an absolutely irrefutable pronouncement about you. I'm going to tell you this with 100 percent certainty: you have known some good and some evil in your life. That is true of everybody. There is no one who has not experienced some good and some evil. Yes, it is the case that some people seem to experience far more of one than the other. Some people are fabulously lucky, happy, and healthy, and they go through their lives that way. Other people seem to be born to misfortune and sorrow. Nevertheless, everyone, from the most fortunate to the most wretched, has known both good and evil.

This answers the question of whether the world fundamentally good or fundamentally evil. The world is not fundamentally good. It's not fundamentally evil. It is a mixture of good and evil. One ancient tradition calls this earth the *mixtus orbis*, the "mixed globe," and the mixture is that of good and evil.

In fact, we can hardly conceive of a world that's at all desirable without some evil in it. People often say that heaven sounds boring: you're up there, playing a harp on a cloud. Another version, where you're sitting in a garden, eating fruit and petting lions and tigers, may be a little more desirable, but in the end it sounds tiresome too.

Are those accurate representations of heaven? I don't think so. But it means we can't even conceive of a world that's at all desirable without some evil in it to provide action or interest.

We are in this mixed world of good and evil, and we are going to experience it. This is the human condition. This is what the German philosopher Martin Heidegger called our *Geworfenheit*, "thrownness." We often feel that we've been thrown into the world unwittingly. As some people say, "I didn't ask to be born." Evil is among the constituents of the universe, perhaps not in an absolute sense, but in the world we have to deal with.

It's probably the case that the unseen world, like the physical world, is populated with all sorts of creatures, friendly, neutral, and unfriendly. They might include some beings that are genuinely malevolent. We have to tread carefully here, because there's an enormous amount of superstitious dread around devils and demons, practically all of which is nonsense.

To begin with, let me go back to a point I made earlier: the human being has the capacity to create living entities through its mind, will, and intention. If so, we can create bad ones as well as good ones. A collective thought form—that is, an idea, a belief created and shared by many—can seem very real indeed. The esoteric term for it is *egregore*. Some egregores can seem very powerful, because they've been nourished by an intense focus of attention over the centuries. Older thought forms, whom nobody is feeding anymore, seem to fade away. That's why the ancient gods worshipped by the Greeks and Romans aren't powerful anymore. They're no longer being fed by attention in the form of worship, so they're gone, except as artistic images.

We have a name for the collective thought form of evil, and it is the *Devil* or *Satan*. It is, I believe, essentially a creation of the human mind. It can appear to be real and have an enormous amount of power; under certain circumstances, it can seem extremely intimidating. But I do not believe it is anything other than a thought form created by the fears, desires, and hatreds of many people over the years.

In fact, most of the gods worshipped over the centuries are merely egregores—including those of Christianity. Why? Because God, the Absolute, the One, this being out of which we all arise, is much larger than any conception we could have of it. At the same time, we think conceptually, so we're going to have a concept of this being: we will fashion images of God willy-nilly, whether in stone or in our minds. It's a good idea, then, not to take your picture of God as an absolute. It is not God; it is merely your concept of God.

Negative entities—many of whom are egregores—are generally produced by extreme fear. You'll notice that some of the more primitive forms of Christianity seem to be obsessed with the Devil and the demons. They're fascinated with these things; they talk about them constantly. This is because these religions are deeply rooted in fear, and fears can seem quite palpable, particularly if they are shared by many. If you look for evil everywhere, you can find it, just as you can look for good everywhere and find it. Hollywood plays upon these fears because people like to get a thrill.

If you feel a negative presence around you, you certainly don't need to be afraid of it. As I said, these things are easily gotten rid of. Here is a biblical verse traditionally used for this purpose: "Let God arise, let his enemies be scattered: let them also that hate him flee before him. As smoke is driven away, so drive them away: as wax melteth before the fire, so let the wicked perish at the presence of God" (Psalm 68:1–2).

If you feel you're being psychically attacked, speak this verse aloud, without fear, with authority, with a spirit of command—even better if you can chant it at full volume. You can say it three times in each direction: north, south, east, and west. If you are a Christian, you may want to make the sign of the cross while saying the verse. You could also make the ritual more elaborate with candles, incense, and other paraphernalia. Details like this are not important except insofar as they intensify the effect within yourself.

Complex, intricate, and elaborate versions of rituals are by no means always the best. In fact, with magic in general, the simpler, the more essential the better, because the more details you have, the more there is to go wrong.

Another method: if you feel a space is negatively charged or something is just not right about it, you can change the energy by making loud, random noises, for example by ringing a bell. Initially ring it in a chaotic, disorganized rhythm to break up the existing energy, then gradually slow down and ring the bell more quietly and rhythmically in order to bring the vibrations into harmony.

Those are very simple, time-honored ways of dispelling negative influences. I don't think you need to call in a priest or specialist. For the most part, you can do it yourself. Actually, the fact that you are doing it yourself makes it all the more powerful.

16

The Pentagram

The pentagram is often seen as the occult symbol par excellence. Popular culture has given it all kinds of sinister meanings that it did not originally have.

Is the pentagram a sign of the Devil? No, not originally. In fact it was, and is, a sacred symbol. We can see this in Johann Wolfgang von Goethe's *Faust*, in a scene where the Devil, Mephistopheles, comes into Faust's study but cannot leave. "A little hindrance prevents me from walking out," he tells Faust. "The wizard's symbol on your threshold."

"The pentagram causes you trouble?" says Faust. He decides to use it to keep Mephistopheles trapped in his study.

But Mephistopheles is clever. He lulls Faust into a delicious reverie. While he sleeps, Mephistopheles charms a rat into gnawing an opening in the figure, enabling him to escape.

Curious, then, that the pentagram should have become a representation of evil.

Although its meanings have many ramifications, in essence the pentagram symbolizes nature, as we can see from this diagram.

Here are the familiar four traditional elements—fire, air, water, earth—along with a fifth element that surpasses and encompasses all of them, here called "spirit" but sometimes known as the "quintessence" (from the Latin *quintus*, "fifth").

Five represents nature in another sense as well—the five senses: sight, hearing, touch, smell, taste.

The pentagram in the form shown above gives, so to speak, the correct orientation: the spirit is at the top, so it is the spirit that directs the rest of the entity. But sometimes the pentagram is shown in inverted form, as below.

This represents humanity in what Christianity calls its fallen state: the spirit is at the bottom, and the physical senses are running the show. Many, perhaps most, people running around let their stomachs and genitals do their thinking for them. This orientation is common, even usual, but in a deeper sense, it is abnormal. It is the opposite of the way human beings are supposed to be.

The pentagram, then, is not a symbol of evil; even in its inverted form, it simply a device for depicting an unfortunate fact about the human condition. Of course there are black magicians and self-proclaimed Satanists who embrace dark meanings for this symbol, but then people will do what they will. (By the way, the details we are discussing here are not widely known, so you will find pentagrams of both types used to mean all sorts of things.)

Simple geometric figures like the pentagram work as symbols. Strictly speaking, a symbol does not have a meaning: *it means itself.* It speaks to the level of mind that goes beyond meaning. All the same, meanings are attached to symbols, sometimes even inverting previous meanings. The swastika, for example, represents ultimate evil for many people today. but that is an accident of history: originally it was a good-luck sign (in fact, its name, from the Sanskrit, means "well-being").

If this brief discussion accomplishes nothing else, at least it should point up the hazards of buying into ready-made popular assumptions, particularly regarding the spiritual path.

17

Witchcraft and Satanism

I'd like to start here by talking about the meaning of a word. This is not academic as you might think. Many people have fought and bled and died over the meanings of words.

The word I want to focus on is *witch* and its derivative, *witchcraft*. They have a number of different meanings in various contexts. If you don't understand how people are using this word, you're going to become confused and in all likelihood upset.

As I've already noted, traditionally the word *witch* was applied to someone who harmed people using occult means—sticking pins in dolls and so forth. *Witch* has come to have a completely different meaning in the present era. Today when people call themselves witches, it usually doesn't have the meaning I've just given.

I'm going to give you a little historical background here, because it will explain a great deal and eliminate many current misunderstandings.

In the early twentieth century, there was a theory that the people, usually women, who were burned for witchcraft in the early modern era (mostly between 1500 and 1650) were not really witches in the sense of doing anything harmful. By this theory, they were adherents of the Old Religion, the pagan religion that existed before Christianity. After Christianity came and tried to stamp the Old Religion out, it went underground. When the church found out about this, they labeled it as witchcraft and Satan worship and persecuted its adherents. Scholars have criticized this theory on a number of grounds, but there is some truth to it. Furthermore, many people, including many modern-day witches, believe it.

Fast forward to 1951, when the British Parliament repealed the Witchcraft Act. Up to that point, it was illegal in Britain to claim you were a witch or to pretend to do anything like witchcraft. (The idea was not that witches could do real harm, but that people making claims of this sort were fraudulent.)

Once this law was repealed, all sorts of people in Britain came to the surface saying that they were witches. Some said they had been following these family traditions for generations sub rosa.

Were these continuations of the Old Religion? Were they modern inventions? This is a matter of dispute. You could read many authoritative books about this subject and still come away not entirely clear about the truth.

Nonetheless, when someone calls herself or himself a witch today, they are usually not thinking of themselves as practitioners of malevolent magic. They are saying that they are following the old nature religion, which has nothing evil about it. It's important to understand this difference.

This revival (or if you prefer, survival) of the Old Religion has come to have a name: *Wicca* (pronounced *wick*-a). Where did it come from? Well, the Old English word for *witch* was spelt *wicca*. That's a male witch. A female witch was a *wicce*.

A thousand years ago, when Old English was spoken and written, the *cc* combination was pronounced as we pronounce *ch*.

So the Old English names were pronounced *witch-a* and *witch-e*. Somehow, rather comically, this mutated into today's *wicka*. And *wicca* was not the name for the practice, which was called *wiccecraefte*—witchcraft.

In any case, many people practice Wicca. *Newsweek* reported in 2018: "With 1.5 million potential practicing witches across the U.S., witchcraft has more followers than the 1.4 million mainline members of the Presbyterian church," formerly one of the mainstays of American religious life.

Today's witches, or Wiccans, employ traditional practices (insofar as anyone can determine what those are). They also use newer practices that were added on later in the spirit of continuing the Old Religion. Celebrations focus on the turning of the seasons—the solstices and equinoxes—or the cross-quarters, the midpoints of the seasons, such as Beltane on May 1, the ancestor of today's May Day, or Samhain (pronounced *sow*-en) on November 1, the precursor to our Halloween. (Many of our holidays, both Christian and secular, can be traced back to pagan roots.)

It's crucial to understand this distinction when people call themselves witches, so that you're not mistaking them for evil people out of fairy tales.

I've known many witches and Wiccans myself. Practically all of the ones I've met are decent, sincere, ethical, often highly educated people with an enormous knowledge of myths and traditions. They are not devil worshippers.

This is an extremely serious point, because a lot of people are practicing this religion in obscure parts of the country, and they are hated and feared by their neighbors because of this misunderstanding.

Are there, then, actual worshippers of Satan? Yes. In 2016, the Italian scholar of religions Massimo Introvigne published *Satanism: A Social History*, a monumental study over six hundred pages long. According to Introvigne, Satanism in its current form started in the court of King Louis XIV of France in the late seventeenth century.

Louis' courtiers were very bored. They had all the luxuries of life, and everybody had long since slept with everybody else. They wanted novelty. A certain unfrocked priest named Étienne Guibourg provided it by performing the Black Mass, an inversion of the Catholic mass: the Lord's Prayer, for example, would be said backwards. The king put up with these hijinks for a while, then decided it was too much, so he put Guibourg in jail, where he died. Since then, this tradition has continued episodically, sometimes with a consciously evil purpose, sometimes for theatrics.

The Satanic impulse can be best understood by looking at George Bernard Shaw's 1897 play *The Devil's Disciple*. It's set among the gloomy Puritans during the American Revolution. The hero, the Devil's Disciple, says in effect, "If these stiff, cruel hypocrites are good people and worship God, I'm standing for the other party." Of course he is the most appealing character in the play. Much of Satanism is inspired by this impulse: "If this sanctimonious, hypocritical religion is worshipping God, give me something else."

Let's move on to 1966, when Anton Szandor LaVey, a man with a flair for the theatrical (his previous jobs included carnival barker) founded the Church of Satan in San Francisco. LaVey's Satanism was ultimately not the kind of devil worship that people imagine it to be. Rather, it was a conscious hedonism. (One major source of his teachings may have been the Playboy Philosophy of Hugh Hefner.) The principles: Satisfy yourself. Realize yourself. Fulfill your own desires. To hell with what society thinks.

LaVey's Church of Satan had an Halloweenish air about it, no doubt because of his carnival background. He became quite successful. He became a consultant to the film *Rosemary's Baby*, which gave birth to the continual stream of Satan horror movies that we've had since. But I don't think he made millions of dollars: his car (with 666 on the license plate) was a Volkswagen Bug.

As you might suspect, LaVey took his Satanism rather lightly: his Satan was more of a personification of the will to self-fulfillment and a conscious, almost principled hedonism. Some of his followers weren't satisfied with this approach. They wanted to take the entity that the Christians know as Satan more seriously. They identified him with the ancient Egyptian god Seth or Set (note the similarities between *Satan* and *Seth*, although the two are not etymologically connected). Seth was not originally an evil god in ancient Egyptian mythology, although he became one over the centuries. He is best known for murdering his brother god Osiris.

Members of this community, called the Temple of Set, believe that this Egyptian deity was turned into the Devil by the Christians. The Temple of Set is very small—with hundreds rather than thousands of members. It preaches a principled self-fulfillment, the desire to become an absolute, immortal self. It has to do with conscious self-affirmation, rather like Nietzsche's will to power—the individual against the mass or society. (It's not surprising that Massimo Introvigne contends that one of the chief influences on the Church of Satan was the aggressive individualism of Ayn Rand.)

The people in these small Satanic sects (to the extent that I have been able to tell) are no less ethical than most—they may be more so. In that case, are there people who do consciously evil practices?

Undoubtedly. Because if you can think of something, someone has tried it, no matter how noble and no matter how vile. But these are best thought of as psychotic aberrations than religions or even cults. In any case, I do not believe that Satanism is a major danger to the spiritual health of humanity, the United States, or anyplace else. And it would be extremely foolish to assume that everything that calls itself magic or witchcraft or even Satanism is evil or harmful.

18

Atlantis and Lost Civilizations

You'll hear and read a great deal about lost continents and lost civilizations. It's hard to sort out truth from fact about these. For most of them, no evidence has ever been found that would satisfy an archaeologist, but as usual, there's more to the picture than meets the skeptical eye. Of these lost continents, Atlantis is the most famous.

The English philosopher Alfred North Whitehead said that all of Western philosophy is a footnote to Plato. Whether that's true or not, all of the lore about Atlantis is a footnote to the great Greek philosopher, because he was the first one to mention it. He discusses Atlantis in two of his dialogues: the *Timaeus* and the *Critias*, which tell a strange story.

According to Plato, the Greek statesman and poet Solon went to Egypt around 600 BC. (Plato was writing a couple of centuries later, around 360 BC.) While Solon was there, he met an Egyptian priest. The priest said, "Solon, you Greeks are children, for you know of one flood only" (the Greeks had a flood myth like the one in the Bible). "In reality, there have been and will be many destructions of humanity, the greatest by fire and flood, the smaller ones by countless other causes, over the ages."

One of these cataclysms had to do with Atlantis. According to Plato's account, it was a large island in the Atlantic Ocean, just beyond what the Greeks call the Pillars of Heracles and what we call the Straits of Gibraltar. These events allegedly took place 9000 years before Solon's time, which would make it 9600 BC.

According to this account, Atlantis had a great and powerful civilization. In fact, they were trying to conquer the whole Mediterranean world, but the Atheneans (Athens was supposedly a city then) stopped them. Then there was an enormous cataclysm. Atlantis sank into the ocean over the space of a day and a night.

The cataclysm hit Greece as well, according to this account. The priest went on to say, "Even you Greeks had much more fertile lands in those days, but now you just have a rocky peninsula," which is basically what Greece is today. "All your best land was lost in the flood that destroyed Atlantis."

Plato's dialogues include what scholars called myths—stories made up to illustrate certain points. Was any truth to Plato's myth of Atlantis? As a matter of fact, Solon was a collateral ancestor of Plato's, and there was regular commerce between Greece and Egypt in those days, so Solon could indeed have gone to Egypt and heard this account, which could have been passed down as a family tradition.

Plato says one extraordinarily striking thing:

There was an island situated in front of the straits which are by you called the Pillars of Heracles; the island [Atlantis] was larger than Libya [Africa] and Asia put together, and was the way to other islands, and from these you might pass to *the whole of the opposite continent* which surrounded the true ocean; for this sea which is within the Straits of Heracles is only a harbour, having a narrow entrance, but that other is a real sea, and the surrounding land may be most truly called a boundless continent. (my emphasis)

Writing around 360 BC, Plato shows knowledge of the American continents on the other side of the Atlantic. I don't know anything in all the rest of classical literature that refers to such a thing. This fact suggests that this myth may not be such a myth after all.

How scientifically valid is the belief in Atlantis? No remains of it have been found under the ocean, but let's look at the timing. According to Plato, Atlantis sank in 9600 BC. What happened around 9700 BC was what geologists call the end of the Pleistocene era and the beginning of the Holocene era, the era we live in now. The Pleistocene was an Ice Age. The northern hemisphere was covered with glaciers. This Ice Age ended at almost exactly the same point when Atlantis supposedly sank. Conceivably these glaciers fell into the ocean, caused the sea levels to rise, and destroyed a civilization.

There's nothing scientifically impossible about this idea. In fact, there's an area in the English Channel called Doggerland. (*Dogger* is a Dutch fishing term.) Doggerland was once above water, providing a land connection between Britain and the continent of Europe. I'm not suggesting Doggerland was Atlantis (it began to sink much later, around 6500 BC), but a lot of land that was above the surface of the ocean in those days is now submerged.

Even fifty years ago, the idea of a lost continent would seem laughable, because science conceived of geological changes in terms of very slow, gradual increments that nobody would notice in a single lifetime.

Geologists since have had to change their thinking. They've realized that many of these changes were, in fact, cataclysmic: they happened abruptly and quickly.

Recently I saw a map of the United States as it conceivably might be in 2100, eighty years from now. There's a little blue ring all the way around the coasts. It includes Seattle, San Francisco, Los Angeles, San Diego, New Orleans, Miami, Washington, New York, and Boston. This ring indicates the land that will be underwater at that point if sea levels continue to rise at current rates. I don't know if that's going to happen, but climate change makes this a plausible scenario. If it comes to pass, who will believe in legends of a New York or a Los Angeles ten thousand years from now?

We can't say that the Atlantis myth is as ridiculous as we might have done a half century ago. This does not constitute proof, but it constitutes enough of a clue to suggest there may have been a civilization of that kind.

Where was Atlantis? In the Atlantic beyond the Pillars of Heracles, beyond the Straits of Gibraltar. In this area is the Horseshoe Seamount chain, which, as its name suggests, is a narrow, horseshoe-shaped series of shoals. Shoals mean that the water there is shallow and these formations are close to the surface. If I were going to look for Atlantis, I would start there.

What do these considerations have to do with us? In the first place, Plato may be right: there are many lost civilizations about which we know nothing. Conventional scholarship generally assumes that there was no civilization as such before 3000 BC, when Egypt and Sumer in Mesopotamia got started; before then, it was the era of Fred Flintstone. If the story of Atlantis is true, even in part, the picture starts to change. It could mean that humanity was more advanced further back in time, tens of thousands of years even, than we believe.

Today there is a curious resistance to looking at this possibility, largely because written texts (from Egypt and Sumer) only go as far back as 3000 BC. But absence of evidence is not evidence of absence.

In recent years a site called Göbekli Tepe was unearthed in Turkey, the location of a civilization dating from around 11,000 BC. That was one civilization that nobody had known about or believed in, so why couldn't there have been many others?

19

The Last Judgment

━━━━━━━━

L et's think a little bit about the Last Judgment. This is a relatively new idea. Most cultures have seen time as cyclical.

A shift began to occur in Judaism in the last centuries before Christ. The Jews long had a tradition of the day of the Lord or the day of Yahweh, which was the Hebrew name for the God they worshipped. This belief became more and more important to the Jews as their history went on; you can see this development in the Old Testament, or the Hebrew Bible.

Originally, the idea was God's covenant with his people: "You obey the law that I've given you," which was called the Torah. It's in the first five books of the Jewish and Christian Bibles. "You obey this law, and things will go well for you in this land that I will give you, but if you don't, bad things will happen to you."

According to the biblical account, the people didn't keep this law terribly well. They started worshiping other gods, and they were punished by being taken over, first by the Assyrians, the great world empire of the eighth century BC, and later by the Babylonians, the Assyrians' successors, in the sixth century BC. The prophets said, "You brought all this on yourselves by your disobeying the Lord, but don't worry, things will come back; Israel will be restored."

The centuries went on, but the balance never seemed to be set right. The Jews started to say, "Yes, we did a lot of things wrong, but what we're suffering seems totally out of proportion to what we've done."

Then a new element came in. The technical term for it is *apocalyptic*: the belief in an apocalypse. We tend to think of apocalypse in terms of an enormous cosmic cataclysm, like a meteor crashing into the earth, but the ancient Jews thought of it as the day of Yahweh, when the balance of good and evil would be set right again.

This day of Yahweh was first envisaged as a time when Israel would be restored. The Jews, many of whom had been in exile since the sixth century BC, would come back to their homeland and would rule it again. It would be a sacred center for the world.

Later on, this concept began to take on more universal dimensions: the dead shall rise again and be judged and time will come to an end. The Hebrews of Old Testament times did not believe in an afterlife in any meaningful sense. They believed in a place called Sheol, which was a shadowy existence in which souls petered out. No good was to be expected in the afterlife. "The dead praise not the Lord, neither any that go down into silence" (Psalm 115:17). The only good you were going to experience was in this life. But if you're not experiencing good in this life, what have you got left?

Again, the answer came in apocalyptic. Everyone will rise again. Everybody will be judged and receive their deserts. That is the origin of the myth of the Last Judgment.

Christianity took this idea on. When I'm talking about Christians here, I mean the Christians who wrote the New Testament. Originally, there were many other different types of Christians: Gnostics, Ebionites, sects who believed all sorts of different things about Jesus. They vanished: we only know them through very minor scraps and the writings of their enemies, so you can imagine how accurate our knowledge is. We can, however, say something about the Christians who wrote the

New Testament because theirs was the version of Christianity that survived.

These Christians believed that the Son of God had come to earth and incarnated in Jesus. In those days, *Son of God* referred to a specific being: Metatron, the Great Angel, who was second only to God himself. It didn't mean the second person of the Trinity, because that concept hadn't even been thought of yet. The Great Angel was "the archangel of many names"—the Son of God, Logos, the Word, the Son of Man. Is this starting to sound familiar? That's who these early Christians thought Jesus was—the incarnation of the Great Angel, the Son of God. After Jesus's death, some of his followers said that he appeared to them. (As we've seen, it's common to have friends and family members appear shortly after their deaths.)

These early Christians believed that Jesus, the Son of God, came down once, broke the powers of this evil world, and would return very soon—within the lifetimes of the people who were then alive.

As I mentioned previously, the Gospels reflect a belief that the Romans would invade Judea, God's judgment would come down upon them, and everything would be good again. That came true only in part. The Romans did come, and they did destroy Jerusalem, but life went on as it had been. Cats, as the saying goes, continued to have kittens. This apocalypse seemed to be deferred indefinitely.

There is a website, whose name I have forgotten, that lists all the years between the first century AD and the present for which somebody somewhere predicted the end of the world. There have been many such years, yet this apocalypse still hasn't come. As I've said, God is not the producer of a B-grade movie. Whatever happens to the world is not going to happen in these simplistic, cartoonish terms. Believing Christians—at least some of them—are still waiting.

20

The Kingdom of God

All of this brings us to the question of the kingdom of God. This is really very funny, because if you are a Christian, you believe that God himself came down to earth; for three years, he taught a few things; then he died on the cross, was resurrected, and ascended. He did this once and only once. If you believe this teaching, you might wish to know what he said while he was down here.

In the Gospels, Jesus talks a great deal about the kingdom of God or the kingdom of heaven. It's the main theme of his teachings. Yet nobody seems to know what these terms mean. If you ask a minister or a priest, or even if you read thick theological works on the subject, you will learn something like this: "The kingdom of God is God's rulership over the world" or "God's imperial rule." Great. That tells us a lot. It is like the answer to an exam written by a student who hasn't done any of the reading or gone to any of the lectures. The theologians have no idea of what the kingdom of God is.

I'm going to suggest to you what the kingdom of God really means. It will explain a great deal about the mysteries of the parables in the Gospels. Let's start with Luke 17:21: "The kingdom of God is within you." I'm translating literally from the Greek, which many modern versions do not. They translate this verse as "The kingdom of God is among you," which is wrong to the point of being dishonest, because that Greek preposition, *entos*, means *within* and not *among*. It's not even ambiguous. The kingdom of God is *within* you, not among you (whatever that could possibly mean).

What, then, is this kingdom of God? It is what I have already discussed in a previous chapter. It is the true Self; it is that in you which says, "I." It has many names. The Kabbalists call it *Tiferet*, which is a Hebrew word for *beauty*. The Hindus call it *atman*. The Buddhists call it *Buddha nature*. There are many others. Sometimes it is called the *watcher*.

Why are there so many names for this Self? Because if it exists, it must exist universally. Therefore it must have been discovered universally, and people will have given their own names to it, with their own colorations.

This, that in you which says, "I," is what's immortal. Not your personality, not your body. All of these things will be gone. There's no point in preserving your body in a tomb to rise on the Last Day, because that's not going to happen; it would be ridiculous and grotesque if it did.

That in you which is the kingdom of God is immortal. What is it like? "The kingdom of heaven is like to a grain of mustard seed" (Matthew 13:31. As a matter of fact, the ideas I'm expressing here go far toward explaining much that is mysterious in the parables of Jesus. You can read more about these in my book *Inner Christianity.*) The real "I" in you is tiny; it does nothing but see or cognize, but the world cannot exist without it. Your world cannot exist without an "I" to apprehend it.

The "I" that sees, that looks out through you as through a telescope, is the only thing about you that's real and true and immortal. It cannot be destroyed, although it can undergo many travails. "The kingdom of heaven suffereth violence, and the violent take it by force" (Matthew 11:12). Like an airplane, this "I" can go through a lot of turbulence, but in the end, it's ultimately unaffected.

Usually you identify with the world that you're experiencing (including your inner world). You become what you behold. But it is possible to detach ourselves from this identification, and this is the point of much spiritual practice.

Understanding and applying this truth in daily life is one of the central themes, if not *the* central theme, of all the great spiritual traditions. I'm using Christian terms here not because I believe Christianity is any better or truer than any other religion, but because I'm speaking to people in the Western world. Western civilization is built on Christianity. You have some idea of Jesus and the Gospels. You have some idea of the myth of Genesis. That's the language I'm using. It's symbolic language, but it is the symbolic language that is most approachable for us. If I were speaking to Muslims or Buddhists or Hindus, I would use completely different terminologies. They would be no better and no worse than these. We should not confuse any one religious form with the truth that is beyond all forms.

This talk about the true "I" can seem rather egotistical: is it really all about me or, should I say, all about "I"? Ultimately not, because here's another piece of the puzzle: that in you which says "I" is, if you follow it back far enough, that which says "I" in everything else.

"We are all one." How many times have you heard that? What could it possibly mean? On the earthly level, we're not all one. You get the girl, I don't. I get the job, you don't. Superficially, the idea that we are all one is utterly ridiculous. It is only true on the deeper levels.

Yet *that which is most intimately "I" is precisely that which what I share most with others.* This quickly starts to get weird. How do you express this concept in ordinary language? The English language itself starts to bend and crack under it, because the English language has not been constructed to reflect this insight.

These considerations help explain much of the paradoxical language of mystical literature. The concept of the ultimate oneness of all of us is true, but it is hard to express in ordinary language. When you try to do so, it starts to sound mysterious and cryptic and paradoxical. Yet we as human beings do feel connected to one another; we have this knowledge intuitively.

In the Kabbalistic tradition, Adam Kadmon is the primordial man, of which we individually are all cells. The Swedish mystic Emanuel Swedenborg referred to this in much the same way as the *maximus homo*, which literally means "the greatest human." This cosmic human is androgynous: it is both male and female. The Bible suggests as much: "God created man in his own image, in the image of God created he him; male and female created he them" (Genesis 1:27).

A Course in Miracles says, "When I am healed, I am not healed alone." Our ultimate unity points to a need for collective awakening, which I will discuss next.

21

The New Age

Today many people are desperate for the coming of a New Age. It's easy to understand why. To put it simply, when the Christian myth of a divine judgment that was supposed to put an end to history began to evaporate, as it has for many educated and intelligent people, it was replaced by the myth of progress and evolution: a constant advancement of humanity. Yet we're coming to discover that progress—which is today understood in an almost entirely technological sense—is rather unsatisfactory.

We have computers in our pockets that are far more powerful than any computer anyone had in 1965.

Smartphones are a triumph. They make our lives easier in many ways, but they haven't made life happier or more fulfilling. In 1900, a play by Anton Chekhov was first performed called *Three Sisters*. In it someone wonders what life will be like when they are dead and buried. One of the other characters says, "When we're dead people will be flying around in balloons, there will be a new style in men's jackets and a sixth sense may be discovered and developed, but life itself won't change, it will still be as difficult and full of mystery and happiness as it is now." That is as true now as it was when Chekhov wrote it a hundred and twenty years ago.

Mere technological progress is not going to save us in the sense of making us feel redeemed and integrated and give us lives that are worthwhile and with meaning. We should be past that fantasy now.

All these factors are a backdrop to the idea of the New Age, a supposed future of spiritual as well as technological evolution. It's sometimes identified with the Age of Aquarius. The concept of the astrological ages is an intricate one. I won't be able to do justice to it here, but to put it briefly, there is a belief, grounded in certain astronomical phenomena, that approximately every 2,200 years or so, mankind passes into a new astrological age. The old age, which we're leaving behind, is the Age of Pisces.

The age before Pisces was that of Aries the ram. In that age—very approximately 2000 BC to AD 1—what was the principal form of religious observance? Animal sacrifice. You could almost say that ancient religion— and this is true of the ancient Jewish religion as well as the ancient pagan religion—consisted of animal sacrifice. The magnificent Temple in Jerusalem had to have an intricate plumbing system to drain off all the blood of the sacrificed animals.

Astrologically, Pisces is associated with religion. That age saw the rise of the great world religions. All of them began to take shape around 600 BC; the last was Islam, which arose after AD 600. Christianity came in the middle: scholars say that Jesus was born sometime between 6 and 4 BC.

The great religions replaced the old religion of Aries: animal sacrifice for the most part came to an end. These religions were the greatness of the Piscean age: they built magnificent cathedrals, mosques, and sanctuaries. They also set out beautiful, intricate, although sometimes incomprehensible theologies.

Today we notice that these religions are losing force. They are gradually fading away. Many people talk about the rise of fundamentalism. I would say that fundamentalism marks the death throes of a religion. Many of the most intelligent and sensible people have left these religions. Who's left? The fanatics. That's why religion seems more fanatical.

This is the end of the Age of Pisces. It is not possible, in my view, to assign a specific year to it, because the ages pass over centuries; we've already seen that the great world religions arose over a period of twelve hundred years.

But I will say this: World War I, which broke out in 1914, came about in part because Germany was building up its navy, and Britain, which at the time had a bigger navy than everybody else combined, didn't like this, so they felt compelled to intervene in a war on the European continent. World War I started in part over sea power. Pisces is a water sign.

Thirty years later, how was World War II won? By air power. D-Day would not have been possible without overwhelming Allied air superiority. The Second World War culminated in the ultimate manifestation of air power—a single bomb that annihilated a city.

The World Wars started over sea power and ended with the triumph of air power. Aquarius, although its symbol is a water bearer, is astrologically an air sign. Naval power is still important, but now air power is supreme. Even in military terms, we have passed over from an age of water to an age of air. Conceivably the World Wars marked the watershed between the ages of Pisces and Aquarius.

Many of the characteristics of our own age are closely associated with Aquarius, such as the hyper-interest in technology. Aquarius is also marked by a certain peculiar kind of idealism that can be summed up in the statement, "I love humanity; it's people I can't stand." Today there's a tremendous amount of idealism and globalism: "Think globally, act locally." Yet Aquarius is also a rather cold, impersonal sign, so the rise in idealism is accompanied by an increasing coldness, mechanicalness, and impersonality in daily life.

We are in the Age of Aquarius. This is what it's supposed to be like. The religion of this age has not yet manifested itself. It may not even look like religion in the sense that we understand it. If a pagan from the time of Julius Caesar came to our era, he would conclude that we are all atheists; he would say, "I don't see any sacrifices to the gods." (The early Christians were accused of atheism for related reasons.) Similarly, this new religion may not look like religion as understood today. What it will be is for the future to hold out.

Up to now I've focused on the negative side of Aquarius, but it has a positive side as well. I myself believe this age will encompass a great deal more open-mindedness, a realization that no truths are absolute—certainly not to the point of fighting over—a greater understanding of humanity as a whole, and a greater tolerance of diversities in lifestyle. Already we have seen many changes.

Nobody twenty-five years ago would have thought that gay marriage would be accepted, much less universal, in the United States today.

In and of themselves, these changes are not going to save us from ourselves. This age has many different characteristics of the previous age, but it's not going to be a utopia. The song "The Age of Aquarius," which came out in 1967, hit a vital nerve, and it expressed this idealism. But the utopia of peace and love that it promised didn't come about, and we shouldn't have expected it to.

In any event, the recognition, however dim, of the fact that you cannot awaken alone leads to a desire for a collective awakening of humanity. I do not believe this awakening has taken place yet. I do believe that possibly, for the first time in history, the human race is *trying* to awaken. The cosmic man has heard the alarm clock. He puts it on snooze. Maybe he wakes up in five minutes; maybe he doesn't. I think that's where we are.

As I've said, I don't believe in prophecies, so I'm not going to make any. I can't say whether this awakening is going to happen, nor could I possibly say what it would entail, because it would certainly mean a world very different from—and better than—the one we have.

Despite the pessimism, wars, inequity, and greed of today, I see efforts toward actualizing this new world. Where they will lead, I can't say.

The medieval prophet Joachim of Fiore said that there was an Age of the Father, which he equated with Old Testament times, the Age of the Son, which he equated with Christianity, and a coming Age of the Holy Spirit, which would be the fulfillment of Christian hope and in which everybody would live in love and peace. This hasn't come yet, but it is something that might come, something that might even be worth working toward.

This Age of the Holy Spirit might include some of the details I've already mentioned, such as greater open-mindedness, but I think it will have to be balanced with intellectual rigor. We cannot submit to the ridiculous fiction that only what we see with our senses is real: that is tantamount to spiritual death. Yet we need to penetrate clearly, insightfully, and without illusions into what we know and experience. The Buddhists have terms for this penetrating clarity of mind, which is, I believe, something worth cultivating.

Perhaps this New Age might work toward a reinforced interest in beauty. Today the American architectural landscape is awful. The buildings are ugly. They're not built to last more than thirty years, and they're not built to look beautiful while they're standing. There's a great deal of natural beauty, but even that is being despoiled in the interest of commercial profit. Looking at Europe, Asia, and other parts of the world, we can see that other civilizations have prized and valued beauty in its own right, not merely for its commercial value. That is utilitarian, commercial beauty, and the United States is suffused with it. This situation may have something to do with the tens of millions of people who are suffering from depression, mental illness, and anxiety.

I think we will have to turn toward beauty, if only for the sake of our inner health. It is mentally healthy to look at beautiful things, whether they are natural or man-made. It is mentally unhealthy to look at ugly things, which are mostly man-made.

At any rate, we are seeing some disruptions not only in the culture, but in the earth—earth changes. No doubt a great deal of climate change is caused by human pollution. Yet the issue may be much more complex. Many say that the earth—Gaia—is a living being in her own right. If so, we have to wonder if our human activities are part of a much larger shifting of the earth itself: that is to say, the earth may be using us, even our environmental desecration, for its own purposes. This is a dangerous idea, because it can turn into a license for anything, but it is a possibility.

In terms of pollution and environmental destruction, I think it's really a lot simpler than it often appears. The human race needs a big mama to come in and tell it, "This place is a dump. Clean it up." Although ideology often gets in the way, it's really as simple as that. It's what every eleven-year-old is told to do by his mother.

Earth changes may be in part natural and in part human-caused, and even the human causes may somehow fit into Gaia's larger purpose. In the end, that doesn't change things. We still have the responsibility to behave decently toward the planet, our fellow humans, and the other species that live with us.

22

Healing

Healing is something that everybody knows how to do and nobody knows how to do. Your body knows how to heal a wound. That's *you*. You know how to heal a wound. It's not part of your conscious mind, but it's still part of your mind. Your doctor doesn't know how to heal a wound—not yours, at any rate. Your doctor knows all about anatomy, blood flow, tissue structure, and many other things, but your doctor doesn't know how to heal your body. Your doctor can't do it for you.

Healing thus remains a subject about which we are in a way very knowledgeable, at the level of our bodily consciousness, and rather ignorant, at the level of our conscious minds. Connecting these two can be difficult.

Modern medicine is remarkably successful at treating certain things but not others. It is not good at treating any ailment that has a psychological or psycho-somatic base. When your doctor has no idea of what is ailing you, he is likely to shrug it off as stress. No doubt stress contributes to illness, yet modern medicine seems designed to increase stress rather than alleviating it.

In fact, a great deal of medicine makes a point of being as unfeeling as possible. You are being shunted around. You may or may not be told what is being done to you or why. You're practically an object for experi-mentation. Often this experimentation—stuffing some chemicals down your throat, shoving others into your veins—works out well enough. All the same, one is left with the question of whether the body would have got-ten better even without these interferences.

Medical science has conceded the role of the mind in healing with what it calls the *placebo effect*. A placebo (from the Latin for "I will please") is usually a sugar pill: it has no pharmaceutical value. But if a doctor gives it to you and tells you it's a wonderful medicine that will cure you, often enough it will. You can read pharmaceutical studies in which the latest wonder drug worked in 60 percent of the cases studied, whereas the placebo given to the control group worked in *only* 40 percent. This is remarkable. An ordinary sugar pill has, so to speak, two-thirds of the healing capacity of a hyperengineered drug.

It gets even stranger. In most of these experiments, the people who were given placebos were told that it was the real thing, or at any rate they didn't know if it was the real thing or not.

But in another experiment, the researchers told the people they were being given placebos. They were actually being told that they were being given ineffective sugar pills, but the pills still worked.

The role of the mind in healing is much greater than is usually acknowledged. Studies have shown that patients' attitudes affect the outcomes even of chronic or terminal illnesses. Optimistic, determined, willful patients are much more likely to recover than those who are resigned or fatalistic or apathetic. Your mindset has an enormous amount to do with whether you're going to get well or not.

Some people go so far as to say that all healing is of the mind. There are many dimensions to that claim, and to a certain extent I agree with it, but that is so intricate a subject that I'm not going to pursue it here.

In any case, much of healing has to do with the mind, and the mind cannot be extracted from it. We then have to ask what is going on in conventional medicine, because if you treat someone like a slab of meat—as I have been and possibly you have—that person may not respond well. Medicine claims to understand this truth but rarely acts on it.

Whether you use conventional or alternative medicine, remember one thing: the doctor or practitioner is working for you. You've hired him. He is not a priest that you've invited in to confer divine grace upon you, or a great authority deigning to spend a perfunctory ten minutes with you at your insurer's expense. Doctors often act that way, and it is in their interest to do so, but in the end, they're your employees. If you're not satisfied, if you don't like or understand what they're doing, you have the right and the duty to yourself to find another doctor.

There is a widespread belief that people who embrace alternative methods such as acupuncture or energy healing are crackpots who don't believe in modern medicine. Very often this is not the case: many of these people have tried modern medicine, but modern medicine couldn't do anything for them. They're turning to these alternatives as a last resort, and sometimes these alternatives help.

In chapter 5, I mentioned acupuncture, which works by regulating the flow of the vital force, or chi, in the body. This flow become obstructed or imbalanced; if so, it needs to be regulated, which is what acupuncture is intended to do. Western science doesn't believe in this life force. Why? I don't know. But because physicians don't even care to admit that there is such a thing, they can't work with it. Consequently, you're going to have to go to another type of specialist to meet this need.

Working with chi, acupuncture operates on a subtler level than ordinary Western medicine, but there are levels that are subtler still. With certain forms of energy healing, the practitioner actually transmits energy from herself to the patient—sometimes even without even touching the patient.

Used by trained and sensitive practitioners, these methods can be extremely valuable. Reiki, a Japanese version, is one common version. Another form, which has gained some acceptance in the medical establishment, is called Therapeutic Touch. There are many others.

Do you have to believe in these practices for them to work? Not necessarily (meaning that the placebo effect cannot explain everything), but as always, a positive mindset is the best approach.

A great deal of healing has to do with the will. I learned this once on a trip to India, when I got the usual tourist's digestive complaint. On one bad night, I had to crawl out every fifteen minutes from under the mosquito netting in a shabby hotel and subject myself to the attacks of insects in the bathroom.

I decided, "I am not going to get sick. I am just not going to get sick." After that night, I went down and I drank a couple of glasses of lassi, the Indian yogurt drink; after that I felt better, and my ailment went away. Maybe it was the miraculous healing properties of lassi, but I have to think that a certain amount of will was involved. It was inconvenient for me to be sick. It was going to be a bother to my traveling companion. It would be unpleasant for me, so I was *not* going to be sick. I got better.

I had had a similar experience several years earlier in Egypt. I'd gotten the same illness; this time a doctor was called in. He gave me some medication, but it didn't work as well as my mere determination (plus lassi) did in India. I was alarmingly sick for weeks afterward.

Pure will, desire—"I refuse to be sick"—can heal. It doesn't have to replace conventional medicine or preventative measures such as diet and exercise, but it can be, perhaps, just as powerful.

Today many people preoccupy themselves with elaborate and intricate diets—vegan, paleo, keto. Often these diets seem like mere hobbies. As far as diet is concerned, I would say that you have to know your own body very well. You have to know what works for you, what is healthy for you, what you can have and what you can't have. Some people can drink alcohol; some people can't or shouldn't. Some people can eat meat; some people can't. It's as simple as that. You should know your own body.

Some people take religious and ethical considerations into account in their diets. I do not believe that
any diet of any sort is more "spiritual" than others. But
of course, the ultimate criterion is going to be your own
choice and your own free will.

Never think of yourself as the victim of either a disease or the medical system. As *A Course in Miracles* says,
"I am not the victim of the world I see." It's better to think
this: "I am faced with problem X, Y, and Z. I have the
inner resources to deal with all these problems. In fact, I
am the solution to my own problems."

23

Reincarnation

We've talked a bit about survival after death. We've seen that the physical body and certain subtler bodies do not survive death or do not survive it for long. We've also seen that the true "I" within us is indestructible. It will go on forever. Nothing can harm it. You don't need to concern yourself with its survival or its care and feeding. It was created by God, and God sustains it.

All that said, many people have questions about the afterlife. What will it be like? Ultimately, this question may be unanswerable, because our conceptions of the afterlife are based on earthly life. Heaven is like an earthly life where everything is wonderful. Hell is like an earthly life where everything is torture.

That's what Christians have tended to believe: you have one lifetime on this earth, after which you will go to an eternity of heaven or hell on the basis of your moral behavior and religious belief. That's theory one.

There's theory two, which has to do with reincarnation: the idea that you will live again—not in some endless eternal state, but by being reborn into a new body on earth; you're going to come back and do it all over again.

There is the third option for the afterlife: once you die, it's over. That's it. End of story.

Those are (with some minor exceptions) the only three possibilities for the afterlife: nothing, heaven or hell, or reincarnation. Which of these is the truth? Or it is a combination of these?

There does seem to be strong evidence for reincarnation. A professor of psychiatry at the University of Virginia Medical School named Ian Stevenson collected many cases suggestive of reincarnation, often having to do with small children who could remember their previous lives clearly and with precise detail.

One striking case was that of a small boy who said he had been a soldier killed in World War II. He remembered the name of his unit and the names of his comrades, and it all checked out. That is very hard to explain by other means. Along with other evidence, it leads me to think there is some truth in this possibility.

Reincarnation is no longer an esoteric idea. Over the past few decades, polls have consistently shown that between 20 and 25 percent of the U.S. population believe in it. That may well include you. Statistically, you have a one in five chance of believing in reincarnation.

Reincarnation and its closely related concept, karma, seem to be a much fairer form of human destiny. By the traditional Christian view, after a few decades of life, which could involve any amount of misfortune or good fortune or any mixture of the two, you're going to be judged on the basis of those few short years, and you are going to be sent either to heaven or hell for eternity. This doesn't seem right, and theological equivocations don't make it look any better. You can talk about the inscrutable justice of God, but this inscrutable justice of God sounds even worse than our highly flawed human sense of justice.

Reincarnation implies a greater cosmic justice. Say you killed someone in a given life. Your karma sets into effect a chain of causes and effects that, according to the theory, means you will be killed in a similar way in a future life. At least this is fair in a way that we can understand. It's a matter of tit for tat. You don't roast for eternity for having done a few bad things on earth. Even the biggest monsters, the cruelest, most depraved, most sadistic beasts, who have destroyed millions of lives—even their crimes are, although enormous, still finite. How could they merit infinite punishment?

The ideas of karma and reincarnation are appealing, plausible, and easy to understand. Furthermore, you yourself may have some sense of a past life. As a matter of fact, a past life regression, which is done in a light hypnotic state, is easy to do and can produce remarkable insights.

Even without a regression, you may have a sense of past lives, a sense that you were someplace else and someone else before. You may be drawn to a particular country or people with whom you have no relation; this may indicate a past life connection.

An esoteric maxim says, neither accept nor reject. If you accept this outlook, it will free you from a great deal of mental torture. I can contemplate the idea of reincarnation. I don't have enough evidence to know if it's true or not true. But I don't have to. My mind can sit with it in equanimity. I think that teachings about the afterlife are best taken in that light.

If the true "I" is immortal and indestructible, what will its future fate be? After death, it may go any number of realms or dimensions. Some may be reborn on earth; some may go on to other realms, for reasons that we may not be able to understand. Swedenborg said that in the afterlife you went to heaven or hell based on your ruling affection. What is your ruling affection? Is it toward good? Is it toward kindness? Is it toward benevolence? If so, conceivably the bad parts will be sifted out, and you will go into a heavenly realm. If not, you'll go into a nastier realm (but not, I think, for eternity).

Swedenborg had visions of heaven and hell, and his description of hell makes it sound like a bad neighborhood, with people fighting and beating each other up all the time. Why would you go there?

I think of hell as a seedy bar. Once or twice, I've gone into bars like this to make a phone call or for some other reason and thought, "Wow! This place is awful. I can't wait to get out of here." But nobody has to be in this bar. Anyone can leave at any time. Even the bartender can get a job at another bar. The clientele are there because they like it there.

That may be what hell is like: as dreadful as it is, you're there because you want to be there. It is a state you create for yourself out of your own hatred, anger, and fear. Because you have all of the power of a son of God, you can make this anger, hatred, and fear seem very real and powerful, particularly to yourself. The question is, what do you want?

Despite their differences, practically all religious traditions agree about one aspect of the afterlife: your behavior and attitudes in this life create a trajectory for what will happen to you next. A lot of these other realms are probably inconceivable to us, and there are no doubt far more of them than we can imagine.

After death, probably the part of you that is immortal will go into the realm for which you have the most affinity. As for punishment, a lot of punishment is self-inflicted. Certainly mental suffering is in many ways self-inflicted even if it seems to be beyond our control. You can free yourself from mental suffering. There are many ways of doing it. Some of them are clinical, psychiatric, psychological; some of them are spiritual; some of them have to do with ethical behavior.

You can set yourself on a positive trajectory. I think if you do, you can be confident that the afterlife will offer hope and promise.

24

Psychedelics and Spirituality

I'd like to give you a little straight talk now about a sub-ject about which there has been very little straight talk: psychedelics, substances like LSD, Ecstasy, peyote, and psilocybin mushrooms. They have been used to produce psychological and spiritual insights (along with the usual recreational purposes).

I myself neither endorse nor condemn the use of these substances. Practically the whole point of this book is to urge you to take responsibility for yourself (which you already have, regardless of what I say; I'm simply reminding you of that fact).

Mystical experiences, which are very common and widespread, have in many cases completely transformed the lives not only of individuals but of civilizations. After all, our civilizations have religious inspirations at their core.

There are psychedelic experiences that are equally mind-blowing. Are they as transformative? Are they legitimate? Is it, in a sense, cheating to use drugs? Many people say that it is, but I'm not so sure. Many traditional societies have used these materials for a long time. One drug that has become recently popular is ayahuasca, which is a drink prepared by the indigenous peoples in the Andes. It tastes like an extremely bitter prune puree. It is very difficult to keep down; in fact, the one time I had it, they gave me a plastic bucket to throw up into. I discovered that ayahuasca wasn't for me, but I've known people who have had transformative experiences on it.

Similarly, there is peyote, which is a traditional Mexican-Indian substance. It's buttons taken from a certain type of cactus. One religious denomination, the Native American Church, uses this in its ceremonies.

So psychedelic substances can be and have been used in a religious context. Is there any context in which these materials are useful today? This is an extremely vexed subject.

LSD was invented accidentally in 1943 by a Swiss chemist, Albert Hoffman, who was looking for something else. He got some of this substance on his finger—because LSD is very strong; you take it in infinitesimal doses—rode his bicycle home, and, without intending to, had the world's first acid trip.

Gradually the drug's properties became known, and in the United States, in the fifties and sixties, it became used therapeutically. People taking it under the guidance of therapists discovered that it helped them resolve their issues. I myself have done this and found it that had great value (although at a certain point it became clear that it was time to stop).

LSD worked so well for this purpose that some therapists simply gave their patients the materials to use on their own. They would take them in their own homes, in familiar settings, and check up with the therapist afterward. All well and good.

In the mid-1960s, the LSD phenomenon started to get out of hand when Timothy Leary started preaching, in effect, that everybody should take it; the authorities should even put it in the drinking water. This freaked people out, to use a term from the time. The federal government objected to this trend and banned LSD in 1967. It was made a Schedule 1 drug, meaning that you couldn't even use it for research purposes.

The reason for the drug's checkered history is quite simple. Therapists who were using it with their patients emphasized what they called *set and setting*. *Set* means, with what intention, what mindset are you going into this experience? For healing, for insight? That's quite different from, "Let's just drop this stuff and see what happens."

Setting was equally important. You were to take LSD in a safe, supportive setting, possibly at home, in the care of someone would answer the door and watch out for you so you wouldn't have to do anything (because you could hardly get up anyway), perhaps playing soothing New Age music.

In that context, psychedelics can be very helpful. Out on the street it was a different story, if only because a lot of the stuff they put out in the street was horribly adulterated. Anything could happen. If you were a bit mentally unstable to begin with, so much the worse for you. You cracked up.

Nevertheless, therapists, psychiatrists, and psychologists have continued to work with patients using psychedelics, often with extremely good results. They don't draw attention to themselves, because these are materials still illegal practically everywhere. But it has been done and it will be done.

Are psychedelics valuable from a psychological or spiritual point of view? I have to write myself out of the psychological side of the discussion, because I am not a professional in this area, and it is not for me to say what materials should or should not be used therapeutically.

To take the subject in another direction, many of these experiences have strongly resemble the mystical experiences described over the ages. A famous study called the Good Friday Experiment was done in Boston in 1962. The researchers took seminarians on Good Friday and gave some of them psilocybin mushrooms; others were given a placebo. The ones who had the mushrooms reported remarkable, beautiful, transformative experiences. The researchers followed up with them five years later, and they still remembered their experience as transformative.

This study I've just described was the subject of an influential article by the scholar of religion Huston Smith; you can easily find it online. Its title is "Do Drugs Have Religious Import?" Huston Smith concluded that these materials were fairly good at inducing religious experience, but may not have been so good at inducing religious lives. That is to say, even if you have a genuine transformative experience, you still have a responsibility to incorporate this insight into your own life and act on it.

Today the psychedelic world is opening up again; even some legal experiments with these materials have been approved. Ayahuasca is widely used. Some people go down to Peru for ayahuasca trips (in both senses of the word). There is some reason for concern here, particularly if you do these things in an indigenous context. If you take ayahuasca among Peruvian Indians and then go back to Manhattan, you may encounter some disjuncture and discomfort, and it may not be easy to integrate what you've learned into your big-city life. And as Huston Smith observed, mystical experience is transformative only if it bears fruit in your life.

A question may come up at this point: how important are mystical experiences in general? What if you don't have them? Does it mean something's wrong? Not necessarily. In fact, quite often, when practitioners start a meditative practice, they will often have amazing mystical experiences and visions. They'll go back to the teacher and report them enthusiastically. And the teacher will say, "Don't worry, it'll pass." Experiences as such are only a minor part of the picture.

One danger of psychedelics, if there is a real danger, has to do with this preoccupation with phenomena—taking experiences, however beautiful, however glorious, however mystical, as a goal in itself. The experience may and sometimes does confer a type of awakening. But the point is not the experience but the awakening.

25

The Brotherhood

With the following subject, we're again going to be dealing with things about which people have many different conceptions and misconceptions: secret brotherhoods and societies.

Here's the negative side: the belief in a secret conspiracy involving all world leaders to subjugate the entire human race and turn us into a race of robots. Certain paranoid theorists refer to this group as the "Illuminati," which has nothing to do with the real Illuminati Order, which existed in the eighteenth century, mostly in Bavaria, between 1776 and 1786. It was started by a law professor named Adam Weishaupt, who wanted to promote liberal ideals in an age when Europe was still run by churches and kings. Unfortunately, the Elector (ruler) of Bavaria didn't approve of this aim and suppressed the Illuminati only a decade after it was founded.

Soon thereafter, right-wing conspiracy theorists—who existed at that time just as they do now—decided that the Illuminati were behind upheavals such as the French Revolution. By and large, these can all be dismissed as crank fantasies, although some people still believe them today.

If you really want to find out about the Illuminati, I recommend a recent book entitled *The Secret School of Wisdom: The Authentic Rituals and Doctrines of the Illuminati*, edited by Josef Wäges and Reinhard Markner (London: Lewis Masonic, 2015). It contains all of the surviving documents of the real Illuminati translated from the German into English. I doubt you will find anything shocking in it, although you may find it rather dull.

Is there a global conspiracy to subjugate everybody? I don't think so. I think there are lots of conspiracies: Coca-Cola is conspiring to dominate the soft drink world. Of course it is, but there are other people and companies who are conspiring in quite the other direction. The idea that there's some unified conspiracy directed by some totally unknown entity seems to me ridiculous.

World events as they are now are not engineered by a global elite. This elite does a lot of engineering, but there are many subgroups with different and opposing interests that counteract one another. As a result, they are far from omnipotent, and the fact that they are human beings means that they are far from omniscient. In short, I don't believe in any unified global conspiracy.

Another legend tells of the Brotherhood, sometimes called the Great White Brotherhood. That is not a racial term. It means *white* in a sense of pure as opposed to *black* in the sense of *impure* (we've seen a similar thing with white and black magic). Nor does *brotherhood* mean that it is open only to men. Does it exist?

We have to be clear about what we mean when we talk about secret societies. By far the most famous secret society is the Freemasons or Masons. Are they a secret society? Yes and no. They have certain teachings, gestures, acts, words, that are conveyed only in Masonic ritual and are only given to initiates. But their existence is by no means a secret. There is a Masonic lodge right in the center of the town I work in, just as there are in most of the towns around me. Their existence is not a secret, although some of their ideas and teachings may be secret.

Even here, however, a great deal of the material has leaked out. If you want to read a description of a Masonic ritual initiation, you can find it online or in a book. That part isn't particularly secret either.

If you read books like this, will you understand what Masonry is about? You can understand a great deal about something externally from its books and records while knowing nothing about it internally. Initiation is meant to connect you with some inner knowing that is embodied in this tradition. You become part of it through the rituals of initiation; that is what initiation means.

Whether the Masons have any deeper truth, I don't know, because I'm not a Mason. But I know enough about Masonry to have great respect for it. And I certainly do not believe that Masons are part of a great international cabal of conspirators aimed at ruling and thwarting humanity. That, again, is right-wing conspiracy theory, and I don't want any part of it.

What, then, is this Brotherhood, if there is such thing? Does it exist on earth? Is it an organization with headquarters in someplace like New York or Geneva? I don't think so. It is not an organization as such. I think the Brotherhood is the collection of human beings, men and women, who are awake at a certain level. The Brotherhood has to do with an awakening to a higher level, with some connection to the true "I." It does not necessarily have to do with joining any formal organization or secret society. It has to do with a rise of consciousness.

These people constitute a brotherhood in the sense that they recognize one another as people who are awake. I had a friend who was riding once on the London Underground. He saw a Buddhist monk. He said, "We noticed each other, because in that particular situation, he was awake, and I was awake." Everybody else was swarming around in the sleep of daily life.

Think about it. You're in a theater with a hundred people, ninety-eight of whom are asleep. You happen to be awake. Another person is awake on the other side of the hall. You're going to notice each other.

I've also spoken about the collective awakening of humanity. Each member of this Brotherhood is, in their own way, committed to this awakening, because they've realized that fundamentally they're the same as everybody else. Beyond a certain point, you can't awaken alone. These are people who are aware of this fact and have committed their lives to it. They may not be mystics in any sense of the word. They may not be ostensibly spiritual. They may not even believe in God. But somehow they know this inner truth and work towards its realization.

If this collective awakening happens, we can hope for a world where people are tolerant, are safe, are taken care of, where you don't have locks on your doors, because nobody would even think to steal from you. You don't have to worry about financial security because even if something goes wrong, you will be taken care of, just out of human decency. Crime would cease to exist, because no one would want to commit crime; they would find it abhorrent. There would be no war, because people would find that abhorrent too.

None of these things are going to be achieved by setting down laws or passing treaties. In 1928, the leading nations of the world signed the Briand-Kellogg Pact, in which they all agreed to reject war as a means of resolving disputes or conflicts. The world's leaders got together and signed a document outlawing war. Eleven years later, World War II broke out, so this effort didn't work out too well. Legislation is necessary in many circumstances, but you cannot legislate inner change. It has to come from within.

The Brotherhood is simply the collection of people who are working in many spheres of life to make this collective awakening happen; their efforts may turn out well or badly, successfully or not. The future may know; we do not.

One important criterion in this work is this: *you do not look for results.* You're not constantly looking back behind you, wondering how you're doing. You do what you do as cleanly and passionately and compassionately as you can and let it go.

I didn't say there wouldn't be results; I said it's not a good idea to look for them. The Bhagavad Gita, the great text of Hindu spirituality, talks about this. You do your work—your dharma, as it's called in the Hindu tradition—without an eye to results, without attention even to praise or blame. You are awake enough to know that in this particular situation, this work has to be done, and you do it simply because it has to be done. This is sometimes called "Work for the Work's sake." You fulfill your task, you walk away, and you say, "Job done. What's next?"

We've been on quite a ride. We've dealt with angels, devils, the Last Judgment, the true Self, psychedelics, lost civilizations, and many things that have puzzled many people. I hope I've cast some light on them for you. Obviously, I don't know everything, but I've looked at these subjects for quite a while and I feel that I can make a few comments.

How would I wrap all this up? Remain open-minded to the realities beyond those we can see and measure. Ideally, this should be reassuring, because you are not trapped in a little three-dimensional box called ordinary reality. At the same time, you are still in it. You have to take it seriously from a commonsense point of view. In short, you have to remain grounded while remaining open to higher dimensions. And you have to remain open without losing your critical faculty.

Above all, you have to take responsibility for yourself and your journey. If you take away nothing else from this book, take away this: you are no longer entitled to blame anyone else for your life. If you're still doing this, it's time to stop. You have to take responsibility for your life and what you make of it. That is an initiation; in fact, the first initiation is about responsibility. Also remember, neither accept nor reject. Keep a flexible mind, a mind that's both critical and open, and remember that there's always further to go.

About the Author

Richard Smoley is an internationally acknowledged authority on the world's esoteric traditions. His books include *Inner Christianity: A Guide to the Esoteric Tradition*, *The Dice Game of Shiva: How Consciousness Creates the Universe*, and *Forbidden Faith: The Secret History of Gnosticism*. A graduate of Harvard and Oxford universities, he is the former editor of *Gnosis: A Journal of the Western Inner Traditions*. Currently he serves as editor of *Quest: Journal of the Theosophical Society in America*. Many of his lectures can be viewed on YouTube.

CPSIA information can be obtained
at www.ICGtesting.com
Printed in the USA
JSHW021321121022
31538JS00010B/72